The Manager's Guide to Benchmarking

Jerome P. Finnigan

The Manager's Guide to Benchmarking

Essential Skills for the New Competitive-Cooperative Economy

Jossey-Bass Publishers • San Francisco

Substantial discounts on bulk quantities of Jossey-Bass books are available to corporations, professional associations, and other organizations. For details and discount information, contact the special sales department at Jossey-Bass Inc., Publishers (415) 433-1740; Fax (800) 605-2665.

For sales outside the United States, please contact your local Simon & Schuster International Office.

 Manufactured in the United States of America on Lyons Falls Pathfinder Tradebook. This paper is acid-free and 100 percent totally chlorine-free.

Library of Congress Cataloging-in-Publication Data

Finnigan, Jerome P.
    The manager's guide to benchmarking: essential skills for the new competitive-cooperative economy / Jerome P. Finnigan.
        p. cm. — (Jossey-Bass business and management series)
    Includes bibliographical references and index.
    ISBN 0-7879-0279-9 (alk. paper)
    1. Benchmarking (Management) I. Title. II. Series.
HD62. 15.F5   1996
658.5'62—dc20   96-15891

FIRST EDITION
HB Printing   10 9 8 7 6 5 4 3 2 1

The Jossey-Bass
Business & Management Series

This book is dedicated to the memory of Norman R. Deets, who for twenty-eight years was my colleague, mentor, and friend. An adult educator who devoted his last years to bringing total quality management to America's schools, Norm was as courageous and worthy as any Nitany Lion who ever lived. His dedication to excellence and his commitment to the people with whom he worked serve as a benchmark for all managers. I will always remember Norm Deets as a true gentleman and a truly gentle man.

This book is also dedicated to Diane Symons, whose natural sagacity, good cheer, and grit provide encouragement and inspiration to her family and friends. An exemplary wife, mother, sister, and aunt, she is most noble as a friend.

Contents

Preface

Looking forward, the next half-century will be a
competitive-cooperative three-way economic game
among Japan, Europe, and the United States. In
jockeying for competitive advantage, they will
force each other to adjust. To prosper mutually,
they will have to cooperate to create a world
economy that works and a global environment that
allows them to survive and to enjoy what they
produce.

                      —*Lester Thurow*, Head to Head

The advent of global competition and the new information economy has led companies like Xerox, Motorola, Federal Express, and AT&T to adopt benchmarking as a key tool for gathering intelligence from both competitors and industry leaders. Their purpose is to identify opportunities for breakthroughs in technology, work processes, and products. In the "competitive-cooperative" economy of the 1990s, as Thurow (1992) puts it, benchmarking offers a structured method for these organizations to share information with one another in their mutual quest for best practices. A growing number of organizations have discovered that by uncovering how the leaders became the best, they can fix their own shortcomings and emulate the leaders' strengths. The benchmarking process allows them to gain superiority by capitalizing on their existing strengths, correcting weaknesses to match the marketplace, and going beyond normal practices to incorporate the best of the best.

In a global information-driven economy, knowledge is not only a strategic asset but also a fluid commodity. It moves between people and organizations despite efforts to control it. Because the new global economy demands that organizations deliver what their customers want when they want it, organizations must be quicker and smarter. The successful organizations of the next century will be more flexible because they will know that in this kind of economy power moves with knowledge and transcends traditional limits. For example, the widespread availability of Internet resources and the emergence of electronic commerce are leading to novel types of organizational structures, knowledge transfer, and innovative market systems. These are facilitating a dramatic speed-up in the process of change itself. Whereas it took over a century to evolve from a farming economy to an industrial society, new types of socioeconomic structures and business models are starting to emerge in very short time cycles. This increased speed and flexibility in the marketplace is putting additional strains and demands on management to produce innovative methods and strategies that can lead to breakthroughs. With benchmarking, it may not be as difficult as was traditionally believed to achieve breakthroughs in technology and operating processes.

In the overview to *Technology and Global Identity*, Brooks and Guile (1987, p. 11) warn that in the United States there is an overemphasis "on creativity, originality, novelty, and sophistication at the leading edge of technological advance." They note that "this overemphasis comes at the expense of what could be called the 'creative imitation' or rapid incremental improvements that the Japanese are especially good at."

Because organizations have to move more quickly in the new economy, they are also losing the luxury of being able to correct mistakes after there is a problem. Instead, they have to learn to do things right the first time! As new technology is changing rapidly, straining most organizations' abilities to keep up, many organizations have learned that benchmarking helps them counter those pressures. They find that the information they gain through bench-marking, which is based on work processes, allows them to better meet their customers' requirements. It focuses them on current market realities rather than on traditional perceptions. With this knowledge they can avoid knee-jerk reactions to changes in the market and embrace goals and objectives that are proactive. In other words, managers who use benchmarking are able to manage based on the facts.

In *Head to Head,* Thurow (1992, p. 260) writes, "A country that wants to win starts by closely studying the competition. The purpose is not emulation but what the business world calls 'bench-marking.' Find those in the world that are best at each aspect of economic performance. Measure your performance against theirs. Understand why they are better. Set yourself the target of first equaling, and then surpassing, their performance."

According to Gerald Miller of the School of Information Science at Simmons College in Boston, because businesses have lost global market share, competitive intelligence skills have become highly sought after over the past decade. For example, the eighteen chapters of the Society of Competitive Intelligence Professionals has grown by about 8 percent every year over the past three years. Jan Herring, vice president of the Futures Group, a market research firm in Washington, D.C., says that companies are setting up competitive intelligence departments. "It's like thirty years ago, when companies were establishing market research," he says (Lee, 1993, p. 9). The reason for this surge in interest in competitive intelligence is that organizations that benchmark are better able to turn their focus away from internal competition toward competition in the marketplace as they gain a concrete understanding of why their competitors are successful. To put it in a nutshell: they benchmark and share data about themselves in order to survive.

In the benchmarking workshops I teach in the United States and abroad, I have heard one story, in one form or another, literally hundreds of times. Here is the story.

My boss asked me to lead a benchmarking study. At first I was afraid when he said he wanted it completed in a month, but he relieved my concerns by explaining that all I had to do was make a few telephone calls and maybe visit a company or two to see what they are doing. So that's what I did, and I submitted my report on time. He was happy and I was happy. But it didn't last. Nothing happened in terms of any substantial improvements in the organization. So, I'm here to learn what we did wrong.

The truth is, neither these people nor their managers understood the process of benchmarking. Benchmarking isn't something you do halfheartedly. Calling a few companies and talking to them about what they've done in a particular area can be helpful but it isn't benchmarking. Indeed, calling that practice *benchmarking* is akin to describing the American troops' landing in Haiti as an invasion. Benchmarking is not a casual telephone call, and it is not a stroll through a plant. Bob Camp, the person most responsible for formalizing benchmarking as a process, refers to that practice as "industrial tourism."

Certainly it is necessary to make telephone calls and visit organizations when you are benchmarking, but the process entails much more. Benchmarking is a continuous, systematic process that requires, among other things, careful preparation, clear goals, strategic plans, team work, data analysis, and the discipline to see a project through. For this reason the benchmarking process must be carefully carried out.

In fact, benchmarking is hard work, often initiated against internal opposition, frequently incremental to one's current tasks, and requiring patience, discipline, and resources. These are all good reasons for avoiding benchmarking, yet the competitive advantages and productivity improvement opportunities to be gained for the organization more than offset benchmarking's inconveniences. For the manager and the project participants, the advantages are the discovery of breakthrough opportunities and process improvements and recognition by their organization as leading-edge experts in intelligence gathering.

Target Audience

It is my hope that managers at all levels of both private and public organizations will take advantage of the benefits of benchmarking. I wrote this book to help you all do so by providing a simple guide that answers the most frequently asked questions about benchmarking. Here are some of the questions:

- What is benchmarking, and what is it not?
- What are the advantages to benchmarking? Is it worth the effort?
- What is the benchmarking process and what investments are required?
- Are there common pitfalls and how can they be avoided?
- How do you select partners for a benchmarking study and get them to share data?
- What is an industry "best practice" and how do you identify it?
- What resources are available to help me?

For the purposes of this book, I have used the term *manager* to include CEOs, administrators, managers, and students of management who are curious about benchmarking. And I don't limit my definition to managers in the private sector alone. Benchmarking is a tool for expanding any organization's access to unique business practices by opening new horizons in planning, target setting, problem solving, work process improvement, and reengineering. Therefore, I think *The Manager's Guide to Benchmarking* will benefit managers in the public sector—from education to the national laboratories and from hospitals to military planning and logistics—just as it will those in industry—from engineering to manufacturing and from planning to human resources.

Purpose of This Book

The purpose of this book is to help managers understand what benchmarking is and what it can do for their organizations. You will learn why benchmarking has become an essential tool in the new global economy and an essential skill for all managers in all kinds of organizations. You will learn how benchmarking can help you to improve your own performance as well as that of your organization. The book describes how to plan and conduct a benchmarking project and how to become an advocate of the process within an organization. It is also a handbook for future reference.

After reading this book, a manager should be able to implement benchmarking in his or her organization and thereby assess the organization's strengths and weaknesses and compare it with the functional leaders. Readers should also expect to understand how to learn from the best by uncovering how they became the best. As a result of such analysis they will be able to fix their organization's shortcomings while emulating the leader's strengths. I believe so strongly in the benchmarking process that I am convinced that a manager who is committed to improve an organization and armed with the knowledge that benchmarking can provide can gain superiority in the field. The first step on the path to becoming an industry leader is reading this book.

Overview of Contents

The Introduction to this book is intended to give the reader an understanding of the process of gathering business intelligence and the reasons that organizations are willing to share information with one other. It covers such issues as how the new economy is affecting traditional management measures of productivity. The introduction focuses on the impact that value and knowledge are having on traditional productivity measures. It looks at the ways in which the "competitive-cooperative" environment has given rise to information sharing and, in particular, benchmarking. Finally, it examines what benchmarking is, what it is not, and what its benefits are. Perhaps most important of all, it suggests how to decide if benchmarking is a management tool that you should use.

Chapter One offers an overview of the benchmarking process. It introduces a four-phase, iterative process model that managers can follow to conduct a benchmarking study. The next four chapters get more specific about initiating and conducting a benchmarking study and putting to best use the data acquired.

Chapter Two describes Phase One: establishing a benchmarking plan. It explains how to determine what to benchmark and whom to benchmark and how to go about selecting partners. It then reviews research methods. Chapter Three describes Phase Two: implementing a benchmarking plan. It discusses establishing a benchmarking team and conducting visits to a benchmarking partner's site. It explains why ethics are so important in benchmarking.

Chapter Four examines Phase Three: analyzing the data gathered. It answers the following questions: What do the data say? Is the competition better? If so, how much better and why? What can now be put into action to improve an operation? Chapter Five presents Phase Four: implementing what was learned. It emphasizes two objectives: integrating the study results into an organization's business operations and taking the actions that will close the performance gaps between the followers and the leaders—or, if you are the leader, the actions that will maintain your position.

Chapter Six discusses what the future holds in the new economy in terms of how benchmarking data will be used in the quest for productivity improvements and organizational effectiveness. This chapter also looks at establishing a culture of learning and change, and how these efforts are supported by benchmarking.

Chapter Seven highlights six key concepts of the new economy that managers will have to focus on if their organizations are to succeed in the future.

Acknowledgments

The act of writing a book is a personal one, but no book—especially one such as *The Manager's Guide to Benchmarking*—could come to be without the help of many individuals and groups. This has been a difficult and challenging task, and I am grateful to many people for their encouragement, assistance, and persistent prodding that I complete the project. Because all of my previous writing efforts have been in collaboration, I did not initially appreciate the challenge of being the lone eagle at the keyboard. I am grateful to my past coauthor, Warren Schmidt, for his friendship, guidance, and encouragement to "go it alone."

I am also grateful to my friends and associates at the University of California, Los Angeles (UCLA), Engineering and Management Program for their support and encouragement, especially Bill Goodin and George Morrisey, who were generous with their time and advice. I am indebted to Bob Andrews for his review and feedback on pedagogy and materials; his feedback was especially helpful in the development of this book. Also, my sometimes co-instructor at UCLA and quality consultant Toro Iura provided timely advice and, as always, cogent criticism.

Were it not for Bill Hicks of Jossey-Bass this book would not exist. It was Bill's original idea, and it was with his blessing that I started assembling my material and researching the field of benchmarking. I wish him well in his new role at the New Lexington Press, a new Jossey-Bass company. But it was Cedric Crocker of Jossey-Bass who gave me the impetus to finish this project. Without Cedric's persistence and creative urging I would still be overwhelmed by my "full plate." His suggestions on structure and flow were invaluable in helping me complete a manuscript of which I am proud. In short, Cedric helped me heed the words of Jack London: "Dig can move more mountains than faith ever dreamed of" (Stone, 1977).

It wouldn't be possible to include everyone who helped with this book if I didn't acknowledge my associates at Xerox, both present and past. First, I must thank the guru of benchmarking, Bob Camp, for his role-model behavior, his seminal writing, and his willingness to share. Without him, I do not believe benchmarking would be as broadly accepted today as it is. I have also to acknowledge the three creators of the first benchmarking training—Bob Edwards, Jules Cochoit, and Jack Kelley. If Bob Camp formalized the benchmarking process, these three legitimized it as a tool that could be learned and replicated.

I am grateful also to the lessons learned from so many others at Xerox, including Bob Osterhoff, John Kelsch, Sy Zivan, Fred Henderson, Joe Cahalan, Vic Muth, Norm Rickard, Jim Sierk, and especially Hal Tragash. I am indebted to Mike Spendolini, both a friend and a colleague, for the powerful contribution of his own work, *The Benchmarking Book* (1992), and for his counsel and encouragement. I am also grateful for the support and friendship of my many friends in Human Resource Management and Organization Development at Xerox, but especially Fred Nichols (and his wife, Sonya), Tom Kayser, Tim Tyler, Paul Carletta, Sam Malone, Frank Angevine, and Bill Skinner. Of course, I acknowledge my friend and mentor Norm Deets, to whom this book is dedicated. I must also express my gratitude for the support of the senior managers of Xerox Corporate Research and Technology with whom I have worked over the past few years: Joe Charlton, Don Post, Chip Holt, Ron Rider, and Herve Gallaire.

If I hadn't had the opportunity to teach benchmarking in a variety of settings I could not have written this book. For the opportunity, encouragement, and professional assistance they offered me, I am grateful to the staff at the UCLA Extension School as well as at the Technology Training Corporation, and their staffs in Los Angeles, Mexico City, and Caracas. Especially important to me were Jim Naphas and Steve Taylor. I am grateful for the advice and inspiration of Nancy Kuhn of the Drew Institute of the American Red Cross. I am especially thankful for the patience and understanding of Dr. Eddi Sutkato of Jakarta's Quality and Productivity Institute. I am equally grateful to Dr. Miguel

A. Cardenas and Nancy Martinez of the International Training Center (ITC) at San Diego State University and to the managers and students throughout Central and South America who have attended ITC's video lectures, especially the students and faculty of the Institute of Puebla.

Without the professional guidance and attention of Cheryl Greenway and Mary Garrett, who managed the production of this book, it would still be a jumble of keystrokes and paper. As in the past, Mary has been a joy to work with. I thank her. I am particularly indebted to Sandra Beris, whose patient editing and recommendations have greatly improved the manuscript.

I thank too my wife, Jo Ann, who has patiently tolerated the lost evenings and weekends. As she celebrated the arrival of my earlier books, after gracefully bearing the pains of their birthing, I look forward to celebrating this delivery with her as well—she has earned it as much as any midwife.

Rancho Palos Verdes, California
May 1996

Jerome P. Finnigan

About the Author

JEROME P. FINNIGAN is human resources manager for Xerox Corporate Research and Technology. He earned his A.B. degree (1959) in English from the University of San Francisco and was an intern in public affairs with the Coro Foundation in 1960. He taught high school English and coached football before entering industry with Pan American Airways at Cape Canaveral, Florida. He joined Xerox in 1966 and has held a variety of human resource positions in Los Angeles and in Rochester, New York.

Finnigan's assignments have largely been in human resource development and organization development. He was an early advocate of quality circles in the late 1970s and was acting quality officer for the printing systems division during Xerox's implementation of total quality. He is a frequent lecturer on total quality management and benchmarking in this country at the University of California, Los Angeles (UCLA), as well as in Latin America.

Finnigan is affiliated with the American Society for Training and Development and the National Alliance for Business. He is past chairman of the California Business Consortium for Management in Education and was a member of the state committee that wrote California's *Strategic Plan for Educational Options in the Twenty-First Century: Roads to the Future*. He also served on the Adult Education Advisory Board, which established California's new adult education strategy. He was also a member of the National Center for Research in Vocation Education committee, which wrote *New Designs for the Comprehensive School*.

He has coauthored two books on total quality—*The Race Without a Finish Line: America's Quest for Total Quality* (1992) and *TQManager: A Practical Guide for Managing in a Total Quality Organization* (1992)—with Warren Schmidt, emeritus professor of the School of Public Administration at UCLA.

Finnigan lives with his wife, Jo Ann, in Rancho Palos Verdes, California.

Competitive Intelligence in the New Economy

The Uses and Benefits of Benchmarking

> Business revolutions are rarely the result of the pull
> of new ideas alone. They also require a push from
> the fear of business annihilation.
> —*William H. Davidow and Michael S. Malone,*
> The Virtual Corporation

In today's world the competition moves too quickly for managers to allow surprises during the heat of battle. In this economic climate an organization does not have the luxury of absorbing many losses before it loses the war. There is no substitute today for winning all of the time. Vince Lombardi said it better than anyone: "Winning is not a sometime thing. You don't win once in a while. You don't do things right once in a while. You do them right all the time. Winning is a habit. Unfortunately, so is losing" (O'Brien, 1987, p. 204).

Horst Schulze, the German-born chief executive officer of the Ritz-Carlton hotels, often tells audiences of the advice his grandfather gave him when, as a sixteen-year-old who had never been away from home before, he left to become an apprentice chef. "You will have to learn to steal—to steal with your eyes," his grandfather said. Rather than a call to crime, it was an admonition *to learn*. Schulze's grandfather told him that no one would offer help because everyone would be in competition with him. Since his formal education had ended, he would only learn by watching others and repeating the things he saw that were successful. Thus his

1

grandfather's counsel, "Keep your eyes open and steal with them." Schulze tells this story to underscore the importance of benchmarking to Ritz-Carlton's total quality effort and to its winning the Malcolm Baldrige National Quality Award in 1992 (Schulze, 1993). Like his grandfather, he offers the recommendation to "steal with your eyes" to his listeners.

Over the past decade, total quality management (TQM) has surged through the manufacturing and service industries of the world. With the advent of TQM, the continuous improvement of processes and products became the basic management approach in many organizations. Leading organizations discovered the power of TQM to improve the way they serve their customers and, ultimately, their competitive results. For many organizations, however, continuous improvement did not lead to the anticipated benefits. This was often because these companies focused on improving things that had no effect on their competitive situation. They invested in insignificant changes rather than improvements that were important for them in order to become better at what they did. In effect, these organizations hadn't learned how to *steal with their eyes*.

The New Global Economy

As a new millennium approaches, public and private organizations around the globe are struggling with far-reaching changes. Their experiences are well beyond anything they have ever had to manage, and there is no end in sight. The indications are that we are in for more change than humans have experienced since the industrial revolution began 150 years ago. In his book *The Work of Nations*, Robert Reich (1992, p. 3) gives us fair warning: "We are living through a transformation that will rearrange the politics and economics of the coming century."

It is not easy to explain with any precision what is happening or forecast with any accuracy the outcome. However, one thing is clear. New, flexible technologies are giving organizations the ability to pursue, on a global scale, a whole new range of competitive options. Organizations around the world are taking advantage of these new opportunities and the effect is the globalization of wealth and competition. Suddenly, organizations that dominated their industries are discovering that their leadership is challenged in ways they never imagined.

In addition, many organizations are finding that their technology investments have quietly given birth to cross-functional operating processes and that their information and planning processes now stretch across their entire enterprise. This free flow of information, together with the introduction of total quality processes and employee empowerment, has created new working relationships, exposing many activities as redundant and superfluous.

Dynamics such as these are spurring organizations to invent new ways of operating by reengineering their structures, finding new ways to measure outcomes, and reevaluating their investments in human resources (HR), often through downsizing and retraining. These kinds of changes are essential because in the developing global economy the mere ability to compete is not sufficient. Organizations have to learn to stretch themselves in order to create new products and define markets that haven't even been conceived of yet. The question for managers who guide their organizations and their people through these transformations is, How can companies create their own successful future? The answer is, They must learn from their environment—from the best and brightest competitors, markets, products, and processes in their industry. They must also broaden the definition of their environment in order to learn from the best practices of other industries, sectors, and societies. The process for doing this is *benchmarking*. This book describes the skills, practices, and techniques that all managers need to help themselves and their companies thrive in the new global economy.

Total Quality and Benchmarking

Quality improvement—that is, continuous improvement and customer satisfaction—and employee involvement are generally accepted as the two basic elements of total quality management.

Why? In order to execute total quality effectively, an organization has to rally its employees to focus on continuous improvement as the means to achieve higher levels of customer satisfaction and productivity. The question becomes, Which continuous improvement efforts should employees focus on? Benchmarking thus becomes a tool for total quality because it provides the means for an organization to identify those business processes that provide an advantage over their competitors. For this reason benchmarking is a key element of any total quality strategy. (See Figure I.1.)

Companies that aspire to world-class status in the new economy have to master benchmarking because it is the best way to guide any continuous improvement process. It helps an organization determine the most important things to improve as well as the best approaches for doing so. Indeed, because the board of examiners for the Baldrige award recognized benchmarking as a key quality tool, it was incorporated in the award evaluation. As Gregory Watson (1992), a benchmarking consultant with the American Productivity and Quality Center notes, the question is no longer *whether* TQM organizations should conduct benchmarking studies but *how* they should conduct them.

Benchmarking: A Definition

At this point it may be helpful to define benchmarking. Although there are many definitions, the one that I find the most useful is from *The Benchmarking Book* by Michael Spendolini (1992, p. 9). (Of course, I may be prejudiced in Michael's favor because he is a close friend and I respect him greatly.) In researching his book, Michael contacted fifty-seven companies and interviewed their internal benchmarking experts to develop his definition. Through a process of finding common terms and then refining his findings with other experts, he arrived at the following definition: "Benchmarking is a continuous systematic process for evaluating the products, services, and work processes of organizations that are recognized as representing best practices for the purpose of organizational improvement."

Figure I.1. Total Quality Management.

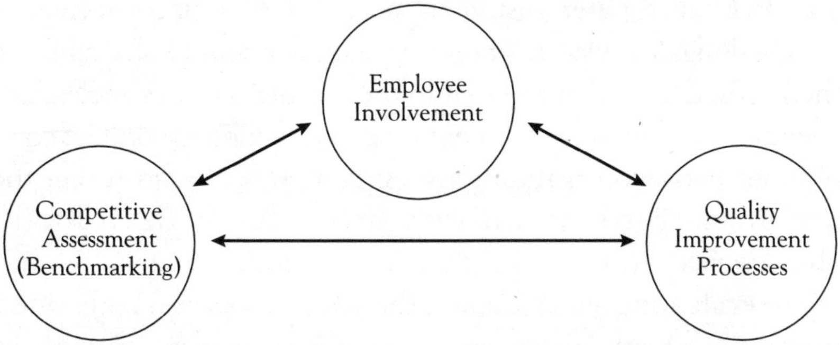

I prefer Michael's definition over others because most organizations and functions—public and private—should be able to relate to it easily. All those who are responsible for an operation will certainly see the value of assuring that the best practices available are incorporated into or matched by their organizations. Also, this definition covers all possible business endeavors, from products to services to support process. It also contains several useful key words, which I explain in the following paragraphs. Here are the key words:

- Evaluation
- Continuous
- Best practices
- Systematic
- Improvement

Evaluation

The first purpose of benchmarking is to evaluate a process. For this reason metrics are necessary; results have to be measured. Measuring is the essence of benchmarking. In fact, the word *benchmarking* derives from land surveying, where a mark on a rock, wall, or tree serves as a reference point for establishing a position or altitude in a topographical survey. In the 1950s, the term began to be used by mainframe computer customers to establish basic performance standards against which a potential supplier could place a bid. In the 1970s, the word migrated into the broader business vocabulary, coming to signify a measurement process by which to conduct comparisons between organizations. At Xerox, we began to use the term to describe comparisons with our competitors. This is why the phrase *competitive benchmarking* is still sometimes used.

In evaluating a benchmark, the focus is always on a business practice or a work process because any improvement can only be accomplished by an organization making adjustments to its current processes. This means that for benchmarking to be an effective evaluation tool it must start with the practice before determining which metric will best measure it. Bob Camp (1989), the original benchmarking guru, stresses that benchmarking metrics are always the result of understanding best practices—and not the other way around.

Continuous

Benchmarking requires continuous measurement because, unfortunately, your competition won't wait for you to catch up with them. Dave Kearns, Xerox Corporation's former CEO, made this point clear in *Prophets in the Dark*, written with David Nadler (1992), in which he described Xerox's implementation of total quality: "We had to establish productivity gains of something like 18 or 19 percent a year for five years just to catch up to the Japanese. And that was if the Japanese continued to improve by about 6 percent a year, which we thought at the time was a reasonable assumption. We would later learn it was nothing of the sort. The Japanese firms managed to improve at a rate of around 12 percent a year" (p. 122). Although the continuous pursuit of measurements may seem like a burden, few professionals object to seeking out the best practices on a constant basis because most know that a continuous exchange of ideas is needed for an industry to improve itself. Today's professionals know that the world is a rapidly changing place and that he or she who hesitates will lose. In his address to the 1992 graduating class of the University of Pennsylvania's Wharton School, Lewis Platt, Hewlett-Packard's chief executive officer, put it this way, "In today's world, it is survival of the quickest" rather than survival of the fittest.

Best Practices

Benchmarking focuses on the most successful activities, which is why benchmarking is more than competitive analysis. The objective is to learn not merely *what* is produced but also *how* it is produced. The issue is not just the product or service but also the process! The Japanese call it *dantotsu*—the best of the best practices, the best of class, the best of breed—regardless of where they are found—in one's own company, one's industry, or outside one's industry. Since the objective is to identify best practices, the best benchmarking partners are not necessarily an organization's direct competitors but the frontrunners, regardless of the industry.

Here's an example. From the time Xerox initiated benchmarking, its benchmark for warehousing and distribution has been L. L. Bean, the recreational clothing distributor. Certainly, L. L. Bean is not a mainstay of the business equipment industry. But in Xerox's judgment it is more efficient at inventory control and delivery to the customer than anyone else in the world.

Systematic

Benchmarking is not a haphazard method of gathering information. Rather it is a systematic, structured, step-by-step process for assessing work methods in the marketplace. As Spendolini (1992, p. 12) points out, "Employees do not have to invent or tailor benchmarking to their particular needs or departmental language. There is consistency among organizational functions and locations as well as a common set of expectations regarding the realistic outcomes of benchmarking." With the kind of intelligence bench-marking provides, organizations can compare their products, ser-vices, and work processes with the best.

Improvement

Benchmarking is a commitment to improvement because the information that is gathered can be used in a variety of ways and have a significant impact on an organization's operations. The find-ings of a benchmarking study can become the basis for short-term or long-term objectives that are consistent with the reality of the marketplace. For this reason they can be used to anticipate business trends or discover opportunities for innovation.

What Benchmarking Isn't

To understand fully what benchmarking is, we have to understand what it isn't. Benchmarking is not a single event—it requires a long-term commitment. It is not a simple process that provides simple answers. On the surface benchmarking may appear simple because it is easy to comprehend but in fact it requires discipline and patience. It also requires a commitment to use what is learned to improve the organization. The most common misconception about benchmarking is that it is a numbers game. As Camp says, "You soon learn that measurements are only a report card; they are nothing more than an indicator that somebody is doing something better than you. They don't tell you what you have to change in order to improve performance" (American Society for Training and Development, 1992, p. 1). Obviously, benchmarking is not quick and easy.

Benchmarking also isn't something one does halfheartedly, that is, not if one really wants results. Karin Kolodziejski, director of strategic human resources programs at Tektronix in Wilsonville, Oregon, puts it this way: "A lot of people claim they are bench-marking when in fact what they are doing is calling a couple of companies and talking to them about what they've done in a particular area. To call that benchmarking is stretching it." So bench-marking is neither a casual telephone call nor a stroll through a plant; Camp calls the latter practice "industrial tourism" (American Society for Training and Development, 1992, p. 1).

Why Organizations Share Their Secrets

About now you are probably asking yourself, Why do companies go outside their own operations when they want to learn about their own operations? And, perhaps more important, why do their competitors share information with them? It is perfectly reasonable to wonder why organizations share their secrets and to be skeptical about the pragmatics of the benchmarking process. Many people looking at benchmarking for the first time doubt that organizations would willingly disclose information about themselves. Nevertheless, many successful organizations do so because they have concluded that in an age of speed and information, gaining accurate insights into the marketplace is worth some sort of reciprocal arrangement (especially since the information about themselves is probably already available somewhere in the public domain, perhaps even on the Net). These organizations have discovered that benchmarking is primarily a process for setting competitive goals that is focused on four objectives:

- To find and comprehend the practices that will help them reach new standards of performance
- To empower their people to move forward to change existing work practices
- To base their goals on an external orientation
- To focus the entire organization on the most critical business goals

The Art of War

More than a thousand years ago the Chinese general Sun Tzu (1963, p. 84) wrote in his treatise *The Art of War:* "Know your enemy and know yourself; in a hundred battles you will never be in peril." Throughout history successful leaders have come to similar conclusions and in this way achieved advantages over their opponents. In truth, solving problems, conducting management battles, and surviving in the marketplace are all forms of the art of war fought by pretty much the same rules as the real thing (Camp, 1989, p. 3). This is the mentality that underlies the practice of espionage and the competitive analysis groups corporations maintain. But intelligence gathering need not be clandestine.

My first job out of college was as a high school teacher and football coach. Since the game of football originated it has been common practice for coaches to teach one another by attending football clinics where they learn all aspects of the game from their most successful peers. As a high school coach I attended these clinics as frequently as I could because doing so was the quickest way to learn how to be successful. The practices these clinics taught weren't considered benchmarking but that is exactly what they were. At one such clinic, I was introduced to a formula for success that has stuck with me, although the author of it has since been forgotten. It looks like this:

$$SR + P = C \times E = S$$

SR stands for self-respect. How do you feel about yourself? Your personal values as well as your opinion of your organization and its vision and mission usually determine the breadth and depth of your self-esteem.

Although self-esteem is important it is not enough—you also need preparation. The P in the equation stands for preparation, knowledge of your opponent's strengths and weaknesses as well as of your own strengths and weaknesses. When we are feeling good about ourselves and know how to correct our weaknesses and build on our strengths, then we can know that we are prepared for our opponent—that at least we can hold our own!

The sum of our self-respect and preparation determines the level of C, our confidence. But this added strength still isn't sufficient: lots of confident individuals and corporations fail. The final determiner of success is the level of E, excitement, that we bring to the fight.

S, success, is thus determined by confidence, which is the sum of self-respect and preparation, multiplied by our excitement.

Benchmarking provides the means for acquiring the knowledge that is needed, understanding how you match up against the competition so you can improve on your weaknesses and make effective plans to capitalize on your strengths. As you will see later on, the truth of this concept is most apparent when the people directly affected by a benchmarking study are engaged in gathering the data because their excitement and enthusiasm can assure success.

The Benefits of Benchmarking

At this point you are probably asking yourself those WIIFM questions. WIIFM is the acronym for "What's in it for me?" The two specific questions you are probably contemplating are, What's in it for my company and what can we hope to accomplish by it? and, If my organization adopts benchmarking, what will it do for me? These questions are appropriate at any time during consideration of benchmarking. According to Camp, there's one "fundamental reason you should do benchmarking: because it works" (Lowe, 1994, p. 12). Uday Karmarkar of the University of Rochester says, "I like to think of it as a strategy of keeping up with the Joneses" (Lowe, 1994, p. 12).

Benefits for the Organization

Benchmarking is first a process for goal setting because its purpose is the discovery and understanding of business practices that can help an organization reach new goals. But goal setting aside, probably the most significant benefit of benchmarking is its motivational worth. When the results of a benchmarking study are fully integrated into the responsibilities, work processes, and reward system of an organization, that organization becomes empowered to validate its objectives and make appropriate changes to work practices based on external facts. The net effect of this is to focus resources on critical business practices and energize the organization to solve basic problems. Benchmarking is particularly powerful when all the people in the organization are engaged in the process because it concentrates attention on the right business goals. There are many ways to describe the benefits of benchmarking for organizations. However, an organization can expect five basic benefits: improving the probability of meeting customer requirements correctly the first time, guaranteeing that best practices are incorporated in its work processes, calibrating true productivity, implementing fact-based goals, and becoming more competitive.

Improving the Probability of Meeting Customer Requirements the First Time. A function's effort to satisfy the customer's requirements comprises many distinct internal processes involving links between suppliers and customers. When these processes are focused only internally, the needs of the end user will likely suffer. Only with an outward focus can the customer's requirements be properly determined, documented, and made good. Benchmarking helps uncover what is needed to accomplish organizational goals by searching out the best practices for efficiently meeting customer requirements. By emulating the work practices of the best performers, an organization can usually improve its own conformance to its customer requirements. As Camp (1989) points out, the industry's best practices would not exist if they were not preferred by end users.

Guaranteeing That Best Practices Are Incorporated into Work Processes. Searching for the best practices at the work process level forces continuous assessment of the external environment. This is why benchmarking is sometimes called *creative imitation.* The purpose of benchmarking is to use what is learned about your organization and your competition as the means for identifying the very best between the two of you and then to exploit this insight as creatively as possible. Also, there can be no more credible foundation for establishing goals than by basing them on the very best processes. When an organization's targets are based on the very best practices available, there can be little internal debate about their veracity.

Calibrating True Productivity. True productivity is the result of employees at all levels of the organization solving real problems. In other words, when employees are concentrating on understanding their outputs and how these outputs satisfy the next person in line in the work process (or the end user), they can focus their activities on satisfying that person's requirements. This can only happen when there is a clear knowledge of what the organization does well and real insight into how other organizations do comparable things. Benchmarking has proven itself to be an accurate process for obtaining such basic data and converting that data into actions that will produce real productivity.

Implementing Fact-Based Goals. To be competitive an organization must certainly understand the competition, but it must also challenge its current way of doing things. This is best done by bringing in new ideas and practices from the outside. Thus, a constant, external search for successful ideas, methods, and practices and the merging of them into the plans and programs of an organization has proven to be a powerful approach to ensuring long-term competitiveness. When the new practices an organization advocates are based on solid facts they form a foundation for building business plans and functional strategies that can be converted into solid operating plan resources and plans.

Becoming More Competitive. Bob Camp (1989) notes that organizations often do not make changes until the pain of competition becomes severe. Too often, by the time the organization feels the pain either life-threatening surgery is necessary or the lead time isn't sufficient to permit catching up. With benchmarking you can see the pain coming. The actual process—of searching externally for strategic data—and the commitment—to use what is learned—are what ultimately result in an organization becoming competitive.

Benefits for Managers

What are the benefits of benchmarking for managers? First, benchmarking can enhance managers' performance by letting them capture the best practices from other industries and incorporate them into their own operations. Second, it provides the people who are involved in the benchmarking process (the manager's employees) both the stimulation and the motivation to improve their performance as their awareness and involvement in process improvement increases. In turn this helps break down their reluctance to change. With these effects alone, any manager should be able to enjoy a more focused, active work group—one that is working on the right things. But benchmarking's greatest value to a manager is discovering new insights by learning about the practices used by others that are better than those currently used. It is a process for finding a better way rather than for reinventing the wheel.

Benchmarking also increases the possibility that a manager will gain a significant breakthrough from a new insight into a process or technology. We can all use a little personal success. Even if you don't find the breakthrough you need, benchmarking is certain to establish a personal network that will offer you potential improvement opportunities.

To find the best practices you have to engage another organization to understand what it does, how it does it, and why it does it. That is what benchmarking is all about. Jeff Miller, professor of operations management at Boston University and author of *Benchmarking Global Manufacturing*, says that benchmarking isn't just a performance evaluation of individuals and groups within one's own company. Rather, he says, it is a way to help "figure out how to learn and improve an organization's effectiveness given that there is a particular strategy" (American Society for Training and Development, 1992, p. 1).

Competitive Intelligence and the Three Types of Benchmarking

Benchmarking is a valuable management tool because it provides a disciplined, logical approach for objectively understanding and assessing an organization's strengths and weaknesses in comparison to the best of the best. Experienced managers of benchmarking organizations know that it is this very awareness within the organization that is the impetus for the development, implementation, and updating of specific action plans that will improve its performance. Ken Karch (1992-1993), director of quality at Weyerhaeuser Company, says: "Benchmarking findings may lead to breakthroughs and innovation. By providing better ways of supplying products and services, it will enhance customer satisfaction. Through its participative nature, it can promote employee empowerment. It will almost certainly stimulate new ways of thinking about, and looking at, the current ways of doing things. The process of consciously searching out better ways of doing things is the essence of productivity improvement and of the learning process itself" (p. 22).

To become an integral part of the management process, benchmarking is ultimately dependent on two attitudes: senior management's backing and your own commitment to using it effectively. The starting point for you as the benchmarking manager is to be certain that you are selecting the most appropriate activities and measures against which to compare yourself, by making a review of the very best competitive intelligence you can procure. Competitive intelligence is defined as "all the information you can legally and ethically identify, locate, and then access" (McConagle, 1992, p. 31).

Once a clear sense of what should and can be benchmarked is gained, the next step is to determine the most appropriate type of benchmarking study to do. The benchmarking process is most commonly classified into three types: *internal, competitive,* and *functional* (sometimes described as "generic benchmarking"). There are advantages and disadvantages to each.

Internal Benchmarking

In many organizations, similar business operations are performed in multiple locations, departments, or divisions. This is especially true of multinationals, which have international operations. For this reason many organizations start their benchmarking activities by comparing business practices internally. Although it is unlikely that a best business practice will be discovered internally, identifying the best internal business practice is nevertheless an excellent starting point. In other words, the benchmarking learning process begins at home. For example, Xerox began benchmarking with its Japanese affiliate, Fuji-Xerox, and today it regularly benchmarks with that firm along with affiliates in Europe such as Rank Xerox and manufacturing operations in Europe, Canada, Brazil, and Aguascalientes, Mexico.

The strongest argument for internal benchmarking is that despite being part of the same organization, differences in geography, organizational focus, and culture almost always results in differences in work processes. As a result of discovering "local innovations" many organizations have been able to obtain swift advantage by transferring that information to other operations within the organization. For example, Kodak launched an internal benchmarking project for its global equipment maintenance. A team looked at internal maintenance measures across the globe and shared the best practices with positive effects. While maintenance response time improved, total costs fell by 7 percent (Lowe, 1994).

Most experts advocate internal benchmarking as the best starting point for an organization that is new to benchmarking. This approach allows an organization to pretest the scope of an external study and to cast its benchmarking objectives in realistic but simple and focused business terms. Speaking about Xerox, Camp (American Society for Training and Development, 1992) said: "We strive to ensure that we understand our own work processes as the baseline to compare ourselves to others" (p. 2). He added, "We have to document our own work processes first. If you don't do that before you visit another company, you'll just come back with a jumble of information and you will have a difficult time making it fit with what you do internally." Miller (American Society for Training and Development, 1992) agreed that you have to look inside your organization before investigating others. A good reason to look internally first, says Miller, is to avoid duplicating what another division in your company has already done: "There is nothing more embarrassing than for one division to announce what they discovered by benchmarking and to have another division say that they've been doing the same thing for three years" (p. 3).

Competitive Benchmarking

Competitive benchmarking is the most widely understood and applied method. It is the easiest for people to grasp because of its focus on the products, services, and work processes of their organization's direct competitors. Employees know that this kind of information is valuable because they know that a competitor's practices affect customers, potential customers, suppliers, and industry watchers. The key advantage to benchmarking your competitors is that they use technologies and processes that are the same or very similar to your own, and the lessons you and a competitor learn from each other are usually fairly easily transferred. In his book *Benchmarking Staff Performance*, Jac Fitz-enz (1993) advises "If you are able to obtain data from competitors, even if the information does not appear to be competitive, it does help you understand your competitive position" (p. 47). For this reason competitors are often willing to join forces to participate in joint projects.

Industry compensation studies are perhaps the most common example of cooperative data sharing with competitors. Another example is the Telecommunications Benchmarking Consortium. This group of eighteen companies—many of them in direct competition with one another, including AT&T, Bell Atlantic, MCI, Ameritech, and GTE—regularly share information with one another (Spendolini, 1992).

General Electric's CEO Jack Welch stresses the importance of competitive benchmarking when he says that GE employees "want to win against the competition because they know that the competition is the enemy and that customers are their only source of job security" (Tichy and Sherman, 1993a, p. 302). Welch also notes the importance of using these data for setting competitive measures: "One thing I've learned is the value of stretching the organization, by setting the bar higher than people think they can go. The standard of performance we use is: be as good as the best in the world. Invariably people find the way to get there, or most of the way. They dream and reach and search. The trick is not to punish those who fall short. If they improve, you reward them—even if they haven't reached the goal. But unless you set the bar high enough, you'll never find out what people can do" (p. 300). In an article he wrote for *Fortune* magazine about the trend for management to establish stretch performance targets, Shawn Tully (1994) wrote: "Employees must be convinced that they're not being asked to do the impossible. Benchmarking is a powerful persuader, showing that factories or labs at other companies—often in other industries—perform at levels that can never be achieved by incremental improvement. Seeing outsiders excel doesn't just teach managers how to, say, cut inventories; it is a potent psychological tool to enlist them in the crusade. If others can do it, they reckon, so can we" (p. 146).

Functional (Generic) Benchmarking

Like competitive benchmarking, functional benchmarking focuses on products, services, and work processes. However, the organizations benchmarked may or may not be direct competitors. The object of functional benchmarking is to uncover the best practice of an organization that is recognized as the leader in a specific area. Functional benchmarking is applied broadly. It is often termed *generic* because it addresses functions and processes that are common to many organizations regardless of industry, including manufacturing, engineering, human resources, marketing, distribution, billing, and payroll, to name a few.

The relationship between Xerox and L. L. Bean is probably the best example of functional benchmarking. By seeking the best practices in warehousing Xerox was able to establish an information-sharing partnership that has benefited both parties. Xerox has improved its logistics and distribution practices while Bean has learned the value of best practices and benchmarking. The Xerox–Bean story is also an example of another advantage of functional benchmarking—breakthroughs. By looking at organizations that are outside of your industry you are certain to find within that function a new approach—a breakthrough—that might apply to your organization. For example, Xerox referred Federal Express to L. L. Bean as a distribution benchmark. While visiting Bean, the Federal Express people discovered that bar coding was being used to manage warehouse inventory and to track shipments. From that study the notion of tracking packages by bar coding was born. Bar coding soon migrated to the airline industry for the tracking of luggage.

Fitz-enz (1993) offers the example of several biotech companies that were having difficulty recruiting chemists, immunologists, and biologists. They approached a recruiting organization that recruited physicists and engineers for electronics companies. By sharing information about their mutual strategies and methods of college recruiting, both parties learned something they were able to apply to their own recruiting efforts. For example, the biotech companies learned about the processing of volume recruiting and the electronics companies learned how to leverage student technical clubs and faculty for referrals.

Today we are seeing this desire for breakthroughs in the benchmarking efforts of organizations looking for reengineering opportunities. These organizations are selecting their benchmarking partners on the basis of their innovative approaches to business processes. By looking at "analogous processes in a variety of industries," they hope to uncover a wealth of applicable ideas for reengineering (Richman and Koontz, 1993, p. 27). Pfizer took this approach in a novel way. The company searched out benchmarking partners that had been in trouble but were now turning the situation around. Pfizer did this because it had found that such companies are more likely than others to be achieving improvements through creative solutions.

Other Ways to Categorize Benchmarking

In addition to classifying benchmarking studies by their subject—that is, internal, competitive, or functional—they may be classified in terms of their goals. They may be considered to be "performance benchmarking, strategic benchmarking, and process benchmarking" (Watson, 1992, p. 10). Classifying benchmarking in this way is helpful because it allows an organization to build its benchmarking capabilities gradually. By starting with performance benchmarking, which requires the fewest resources, you can become familiar with the process with a minimal investment. When you are comfortable with gathering data and using the information you acquire, you can go on to build partnerships with a specific set of companies to understand better the strategic issues. Finally, when your organization becomes capable and confident at adapting benchmarking information, you can initiate a team-training program to help your work teams conduct their own process benchmarking studies. (We'll talk more about the use of teams later.)

Performance Benchmarking

If the purpose of a benchmarking study is to identify whose performance is better—based on established measures of productivity—performance benchmarking is the easiest kind of study. The performance category of benchmarking includes all research-based studies, whether the data come from competitors or functional leaders. Performance benchmarking requires the least resource support because it relies on the analysis of data from database searches and surveys that can be conducted by an experienced librarian or a market research professional. Most organizations also find performance research a good way to begin benchmarking because it doesn't require contact with the organizations being benchmarked. That, in turn, means no costly plant visits. In addition, on the basis of such research an expanded study with site visits and more in-depth inquiry can easily be made.

Strategic Benchmarking

In strategic benchmarking the focus goes beyond performance leadership to examine nonindustry leaders in an attempt to identify significant trends that may provide insight into potential improvement opportunities. Strategic benchmarking is usually done by establishing benchmarking alliances with a limited number of noncompeting businesses. GE is probably the most successful employer of this method, using such alliances with fewer than twenty internationally recognized businesses. Strategic benchmarking has become increasingly popular because it requires only a limited investment—usually a small professional team with sufficient funding and time to establish long-term continuity. As already noted, for many years organizations studying industry compensation practices have taken this approach.

Process Benchmarking

Process benchmarking requires the highest commitment and experience. It means seeking the best practices through face-to-face studies and observations of key business processes, regardless of who the best practices candidate may be. Because process benchmarking requires the participation of subject matter experts, the owner of a process and the process work team (the people actually doing the work) have to be involved in the study. In addition to dedicated support, process benchmarking requires extensive training, site visits, and travel expense; it will also probably lead to extensive process changes. Although the investments are great, so are the returns.

The Xerox Model

It is important to realize that benchmarking is not new and that it is practiced by many successful organizations. In their book, *Made in America: Regaining the Productive Edge*, Michael Dertouzos and colleagues (1989) wrote: "A characteristic of all the best-practice American firms we observed, large or small, is an emphasis on competitive benchmarking: comparing the performance of their products and work processes with those of the world leaders in order to achieve improvement and to measure progress" (p. 119). It is largely due to the success of Xerox, which began "evaluating" its competition as early as 1976, that benchmarking has become a widely accepted quality tool. Because of increasing competitive pressure, especially from the Japanese, Xerox began to pioneer the formal benchmarking process in 1979. Based on the data gathered by this process, Xerox decided to pursue a total quality strategy and started to establish internal targets based on outside comparisons. In fact, Xerox's total quality strategy is based on an interdependent trilogy of three things: quality improvement, employee involvement, and benchmarking. By 1981 Xerox had adopted benchmarking as a corporatewide effort. At the 1983 annual meeting of shareholders, CEO Dave Kearns announced that his number one priority was to achieve "leadership through quality" (Camp, 1989, p. 7) and that benchmarking would lead the way by providing the targets to be met. Kearns (Kearns and Nadler, 1992) says of benchmarking that it was "the first thing we did to get Xerox on its feet and moving again" (p. 123). Kearns adds that benchmarking had "spread like wildfire" and that "we were doing more of it than anybody. We were fast closing in on our goal of having every department in the company measuring its performance against similar operations at other companies—even lawyers and strategic planners" (p. 238). As a result, Xerox not only became more competitive but, by the mid 1980s, recovered all of the market share that it had previously lost to the Japanese.

Xerox continued to develop its benchmarking concept throughout the 1980s. Camp, Sy Zivan, Cary Kimmel, John Kelsch, and many others contributed to formalization of the process into a ten-step model (see Figure I.2). In 1986, at Xerox's El Segundo, California, operations, Bob Edwards and Jules Cochoit, education and training, joined with Jack Kelly, finance, to develop the first benchmarking training curriculum. This course allowed Xerox to introduce the process to a broad representation of employees, customers, and suppliers. Today Xerox's budgets and operating targets are based on assessments made outside the corporation.

By 1983 many other companies, including AT&T, GTE, and IBM, had begun conducting benchmarking studies. But as Spendolini (1992) points out, it wasn't until the end of that decade that benchmarking took off. It wasn't until then that literature and consultants became available to teach and guide users of the process. The watershed year was 1989 when Bob Camp's definitive book on the subject, *Benchmarking: The Search for Industry Best Practices*, was published. Camp's book quickly became a best-seller because it was the first comprehensive explanation of the subject. It became a Bible for most benchmarking practitioners and beginners. Today, their numbers continue to grow. In a survey of 203 companies, the Conference Board (1993) learned that 67 percent of the respondents had at least some benchmarking experience, while nearly 75 percent reported success in benchmarking applications.

The Conference Board survey also indicated that a majority of the companies responding had experienced tangible benefits from benchmarking. As an example, 59 percent said that they had reduced costs as a result of benchmarking; 53 percent reported that

**Figure I.2. The Xerox Ten-Step
Benchmarking Process Model.**

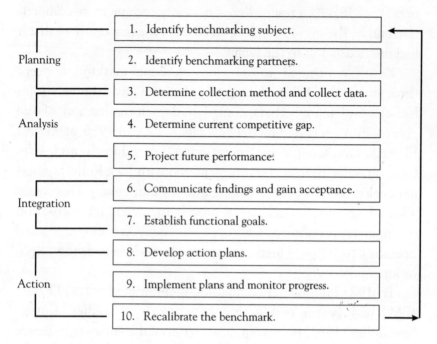

Source: Xerox Corporation. Used by permission.

they had improved customer service; 50 percent indicated that
their benchmarking experiences had improved quality; and 51 percent claimed that they had improved productivity. Positive results
like this have led to the formation of the International Benchmarking Clearinghouse (IBC), a service of the American Productivity and Quality Center (APQC). IBC is a consortium of over
ninety companies that promotes, facilitates, and improves benchmarking as a business tool. The brainchild of C. Jackson Grayson
and Carla O'Dell, IBC was spearheaded by Marty Russell, now a
benchmarking consultant in California. IBC is a networking organization that provides a repository of benchmarking information
and a center for sharing expertise.

Benchmarking Success Stories

The steady growth of benchmarking as a management tool is a testament to its power to provide tangible benefits for participating organizations. To illustrate the power of benchmarking, I'd like to share a few success stories with you.

Francis Cabot Lowell: An Early Case

In 1810, thirty-five-year-old Francis Cabot Lowell, a Boston merchant, traveled to England for his health. While in Lancashire, the center of England's textile industry, he was impressed both by the textile operations he saw and by the contribution the industry was making to the wealth of the country as a whole. He was particularly impressed with the textile machinery there. After much reflection upon his observations, Lowell decided that he could improve upon British manufacturing technology. He also believed that most British mills were poorly laid out and failed to utilize adequately their labor. When he returned to Massachusetts during the War of 1812, he was determined to become a textile manufacturer. He joined forces with Paul Moody, a friend and a mechanical genius, and drawing on his memory of Lancashire, went on to invent the first power loom. With his brother-in-law, Patrick Tracy Jackson, and another friend, Nathan Appleton, Lowell then founded the Boston Manufacturing Company in Waltham, Massachusetts. In 1814 he built a plant that was the first in the world to house all stages of cotton manufacturing under one roof. Most notably, the plant used less labor-intensive methods than its English competitors. With plans to move the company's operations to a small village called East Chelmsford, Lowell not only designed the layout of the new manufacturing facilities but also planned for expansion of the city to provide worker housing, schools, stores, and recreational facilities. Lowell died in 1817 but the first of the several new plants he planned opened in 1823. Both his enterprise and the community thrived and in 1826 the city was renamed in his honor. By

1830 Lowell, Massachusetts, had become America's largest manufacturing complex; by 1840 it was America's fastest-growing city. Although his was probably not the world's first benchmarking study, Lowell's may well have been the first for America.

Toyota/General Motors/NUMMI

In 1950 Toyota Motor Corporation sent industrial engineer Eliji Toyoda to the United States to study automobile manufacturing and engineering processes. Toyoda visited General Motors (GM), Ford, Chrysler, and Studebaker. On the basis of his observations he concluded that GM had the superior manufacturing technology and that it could not be easily improved upon. But Toyoda also discovered that GM maintained large inventories of parts and subassemblies. He decided that if Toyota could capitalize on GM's manufacturing technology while avoiding that company's material costs, it would have a price advantage in the American market. Thus the just-in-time manufacturing strategy was born and Toyota's assault upon the American automobile market launched. In due course Eliji Toyoda became chairman of Toyota. In 1984 GM entered into a manufacturing joint venture with Toyota at Fremont, California, named New United Motor Manufacturing Inc. (NUMMI). Robert Stempel, who became GM's CEO, said when the joint venture was announced that GM's "main reason for this joint venture is to see how Toyota runs a factory" (California Manufacturers Association, 1994, p. 1).

Thus, the benchmarking process that Eliji Toyoda started had come full circle. Ten years after its founding NUMMI was the lone survivor among eight car manufacturing operations in California, employing 4,300 "team members" who produced some 330,000 vehicles a year, including Chevrolet Geo Prizms, Toyota Corolla sedans, and Toyota compact trucks. In May 1994, to commemorate ten years of operations, NUMMI presented ten vehicles to the state of California. The cars and trucks were accepted by Governor Pete Wilson in a formal ceremony and donated to the staffs of selected people-oriented agencies. Toyota's president, Tatsuro Toyoda, said, "On the occasion of New United Motor's tenth anniversary, we could think of no more appropriate gift from GM and Toyota to the community of California than ten vehicles built with pride here in California by the NUMMI team" (California Manufacturers Association, 1994, p. 1). In *Quality or Else*, Lloyd Dobyns and Clare Crawford-Mason (1991) reported that GM's top managers have accepted NUMMI's success so enthusiastically that NUMMI "limits the number of GM officials who can visit the plant" because the platoons of visitors studying the NUMMI quality system were interfering with that system (p. 113).

The most notable success for GM has been its ability to apply much of what it learned at NUMMI to its Saturn plant in Spring Hill, Tennessee. Saturn produced its first cars in 1990. Five years of feedback from customers indicates that Saturn models perform as well as the Japanese models they were built to rival. The reports from Saturn suggest that both workers and managers are thriving amid the less rigid work processes copied from NUMMI (Bowles and Hammond, 1991).

Xerox

Benchmarking at Xerox first started in the corporation's Rochester, New York, manufacturing operations division in 1979 as part of an effort to assess its unit manufacturing costs (UMC). Tucker, Zivan, and Camp (1987, p. 8) put it this way in a *Harvard Business Review* article: Xerox had become "uncomfortably aware of the extremely low prices of Japanese plain-paper copiers" and wanted "to determine whether their Japanese counterparts' relative costs were as low as their relative prices." Part of the UMC study involved an analysis of copiers produced by Xerox's Japanese affiliate, Fuji-Xerox. This data exchange later extended to other Japanese manufacturers like Canon, Minolta, and Toyota; when this happened comprehensive benchmarking was formalized. As previously noted, Xerox's investigations were strategically significant because they confirmed that the company's U.S. manufacturing costs were higher than those of its Japanese competitors. In fact, some of these competitors were selling their copiers for what it cost Xerox to make a comparable machine. As the article noted, "Discarding their standard budgeting processes, U.S. manufacturing operations adopted the lower Japanese costs as targets for driving their own business plans. Top management, gratified with the results, directed all units and cost centers in the corporation to use benchmarking" (Tucker, Zivan, and Camp, 1987, p. 8). At the time, Kearns defined this approach as the "continuous process of measuring our products, services, and practices against our toughest competitors or those companies renowned as leaders. Our goal is superiority in all areas—quality, product reliability, and cost" (Kearns and Nadler, 1992, pp. 123–124).

Perhaps the most significant benchmarking effort Xerox conducted was that with L. L. Bean. The effort was started by Xerox's logistics and distribution unit in early 1981 when Bob Camp was assigned part time "to come up with a suitable noncompetitor to benchmark in the warehousing and materials handling area" (Tucker, Zivan, and Camp, 1987, p. 9). Xerox had just built a high-rise automated storage and retrieval system (ASRS) for raw materials and parts. ASRS was located in the same facility as a large product distribution center but an internal study indicated that such a large capital investment could not be justified for finished goods. Camp's study was intended to bring an external perspective to the issue. He examined trade journals, talked with professional associations and consultants, and developed a list of companies with the best reputations for distribution. Then he combed the list for organizations that possessed generic product characteristics and service values similar to those of Xerox. By fall he selected Bean and in a memo to management gave the reasons for his recommendation. He said that Bean's warehousing design was well thought out and chosen with the "full participation of the hourly work force" (Tucker, Zivan, and Camp, 1987, p. 9). Three months later Camp, joined by a headquarters distribution manager and a field distribution manager, visited Bean at Freeport, Maine. The group learned that Bean's warehousing system had these characteristics: materials were arranged so that fast-moving items were closest to the picker route; incoming orders were sorted and released throughout the day to minimize traveling distance; incentive bonuses were based on picker productivity. Camp also learned that Bean had plans to implement automated data capture by the use of bar coding. Because Bean's system was labor-intensive it was easily adapted to Xerox's purposes and Xerox was able to incorporate some of the practices in automating its own warehousing. As noted earlier, Bean was able to benefit, too, because after it saw Xerox's success it adopted benchmarking as part of its own planning processes. Kearns recalls that Bob Camp didn't stop there: "He went on to benchmark American Hospital Supply because they moved a lot of small things around the country fast and so did we. He benchmarked Caterpillar because they moved big things around the country fast and so did we" (Kearns and Nadler, 1992, pp. 238–239). To follow up on Camp's efforts, Xerox published a pamphlet on benchmarking for all employees. The pamphlet contained the rudiments of benchmarking (including Camp's process model) and stated, "We must understand that Xerox does not, and cannot, always have the best answer to every problem we encounter" (p. 239).

Today benchmarking at Xerox is the external source of facts for determining tactical and strategic plans. Wayland Hicks, a former Xerox executive vice president, described the 1973 to 1982 period at Xerox as a "chapter of a bad book that you're not going to read twice" (Chakravarty, 1994, p. 73). The success of the turnaround is best expressed by the fact that Xerox is the only company in the world to have won all three major quality awards: Japan's Deming prize, America's Baldrige award, and the European quality award.

Motorola

An even more dramatic example of benchmarking applications is the experience of Motorola's Bandit plant at Fort Boynton Beach, Florida. The Bandit was a pager product initiated by Motorola in the late 1980s under a unique set of engineering and manufacturing rules. First, the team was told to abandon the start-from-scratch approach and utilize whatever applicable designs and parts already existed on Motorola's shelves. They were also told that the traditional resistance to ideas and designs developed outside the organization—what is sometimes called the not-invented-here syndrome—would have to be put aside. Instead, the twenty-four-person Bandit product development team was encouraged to use *anybody's* ideas. So the team visited the best engineering and manufacturing organizations in the world and "borrowed" liberally from what was seen. The team visited "factories that did everything from assembling cars to grinding optical fiber lenses" and met with suppliers, university professors, and customers (Dobyns and Crawford-Mason, 1991, p. 148). In fact, the team came up with the name *bandit* because it had readily used every applicable idea found with resounding success. Made up of product design engineers, process developers, tooling designers, software specialists, and marketing and financial people, the Bandit team benchmarked Honda's just-in-time manufacturing process, Seiko's robotics techniques, and other Motorola operations' computer-integrated manufacturing (CIM) techniques. The ideas garnered from benchmarking and incorporated in both the product and the plant read like a CEO's wish list of advanced competitiveness techniques including simultaneous engineering, design for manufacturability and assembly, and flexible manufacturing (Bowles and Hammond, 1991). The Bandit pager was a personalized product, requiring a plant that could produce a lot size of one, which is exactly what the Fort Boynton Beach plant did. What would have been a thirty-day production process in another Motorola plant took only twenty-eight minutes in this "factory of the future." Perhaps even more significant, the entire project was completed in eighteen months whereas doing things the accepted Motorola way would have taken thirty-six. Motorola's Bandit is thus a prime example of a product designed and built using key data from benchmarking. Today Fort Boynton Beach is the automated production home to the "grandchildren" of the original programmable pager.

AT&T

In 1987, AT&T began an effort to benchmark its software development process capability. The company first baselined its software development process characteristics and performance for about twenty-five AT&T products against standard industry assessment tools. The benchmarking data revealed that its best products compared favorably with its benchmarking partners but that there was also a great degree of process variability within AT&T software products. In addition, as part of its approach, it held formal exchanges with companies that dealt successfully with benchmarking. AT&T learned a good deal from Hewlett-Packard and others about the use of "best current practices" (BCPs) as a means to motivate process uniformity and performance improvement across a diverse organization. This experience led Bell Laboratories to establish process teams to guide the development of BCPs for AT&T's key R&D process steps. A formal BCP process was launched in 1988. Since then, a dozen practices have been developed and implemented. To date, BCPs have been well received within AT&T Bell Laboratories, and many organizations have become actively involved in suggesting and investigating new practices. In 1990 alone Bell Laboratories personnel engaged in nearly three hundred formal technical exchanges (scientist-to-scientist exchanges, not all of which were benchmarking) with other companies. These experiences reaffirmed the value of a strong focus on information sharing and standard benchmarking practices to improve the effectiveness and efficiency of product development. AT&T also learned from other companies how to manage and support its benchmarking efforts better and share the information collected. It has used these findings to improve its benchmarking approach. Thomas Bean and Jacques Gros (1992) have identified six benefits of Bell Labs' benchmarking efforts (p. 32):

1. They establish expectation levels of success by showing what other companies have achieved.

2. They provide a source of ideas for process improvements.

3. They provide approaches for implementing process improvements.

4. They provide the performance levels of industry leaders and competitors to motivate change.

5. They provide role models for cultural change.

6. They serve as input for strategic planning processes, both technical and business.

BCP support includes a detailed handbook geared to AT&T practices, introductory seminars, operational training, and hands-on consulting support for project teams that are beginning to apply the methods to help jump-start their study. AT&T believes in the power of benchmarking so much that it created a group of fifteen "experts" to assist its numerous divisions in benchmarking. Dennis Percher, a benchmarking consultant and trainer for AT&T's benchmarking group describes its role this way, "We help people focus on what they want to benchmark, and to select companies. We facilitate the visits and analyze the information. Basically, we work with them through the whole process to the point where they make recommendations and implement changes" (American Society for Training and Development, 1992, p. 2). When a division decides to benchmark, its manager usually calls upon an expert and explains what he wants to do. Percher says that they engage in an extensive dialogue to determine what the division really wants to benchmark. The object is to narrow the focus on the benchmark and then facilitate their use of AT&T's nine-step benchmarking process. Spendolini reports that AT&T maintains an information resource staffed by library specialists "who offer a variety of information-gathering and analysis services" (1992, p. 139). The AT&T experts don't do the benchmarking for their clients but only advise them. "I'm not an expert in their area," says Percher. "I don't know their process well enough, so they have to be involved. I wouldn't want to do it myself and then hand over a report. I want them to see these places and to establish partnerships on an ongoing basis with their counterparts in other organizations" (American Society for Training and Development, 1992, p. 2). In addition to helping in benchmarking activities, the AT&T expert group also conducts training courses. It offers a two-day training course for the people who will be doing the actual benchmarking and a half-day course for the sponsor or the person who is allocating the money for the project. Also provided is a two-hour executive overview for top management. "Often I try to get that upper level of management to come to training because I want them to be a critical part of the process supporting benchmarking," says Percher (American Society for Training and Development, 1992, p. 2). Like Xerox, in addition to the training, AT&T provides all its employees a benchmarking handbook that describes the process efficiently but succinctly, and includes detailed checklists to help guide teams. Bean and Gros (1992) go on to point out that "benchmarking played a significant role in efforts undertaken by AT&T's consumer products (CP) business unit to improve its rate of new product introduction" (p. 34). The analysis of R&D performance within their industry helped CP discover shorter best-in-class design cycles that it was able to incorporate in their own operations.

General Electric

Ever since Thomas Edison founded GE over a hundred years ago the company has been known as an organization that produces good ideas for themselves and their customers. But not long ago there was growing concern that GE had come to think of itself as the *only* source of a good idea. Judging that "one of GE's great weaknesses always was its susceptibility to the not-invented-here syndrome" CEO Jack Welch assigned Michael Frazier of GE's business development group to develop a list of organizations from which the company might learn something (Tichy and Sherman,

1993b, pp. 31–32). Frazier formed a best practices team of ten members who spent a full year collecting data on-site on nine companies, including Ford Motor Company, Hewlett-Packard, and Chapperell Steel. "They were seeking answers to the question, What is the secret of your success?" (Tichy and Sherman, 1993b, p. 32). In the team's report, it was concluded that the success of the productivity leaders depended upon six common characteristics:

1. They managed process rather than people with an emphasis on *how* rather than *how much*.
2. They used benchmarking and process maps to identify opportunities for improvement.
3. They implemented continuous improvement based on incremental gains.
4. They used customer satisfaction as the main gauge of performance.
5. Their productivity emphasis was based on high-quality new products designed for efficient manufacturing.
6. They treated suppliers as partners.

Of particular value were the "war stories" included in the report. One such story was about a leading producer of washing machines in Japan. By 1984 this company had decided that, because of demographic changes, its market would segment into niches. Management concluded that they needed to switch from production of a few high-volume machines to a broader selection that would sell at lower volumes. The formidable task was to accomplish the switch without creating problems on the assembly line. The solution was a flexible production system designed to respond directly to the ebb and flow of sales. "In five years the company tripled the number of new washer models it introduced. The washer factory became accustomed to eleven model changes per day versus two and a half per day in 1985. Spending $2 million to $3 million each year to make all the changes, the business doubled both its manufacturing capacity and the dollar amount of sales per employee. At the same time, quality dramatically improved" (Tichy and Sherman, 1993b, p. 250). After the best practices team's report Welch ordered that best practices be spread throughout GE. Today he frequently quotes Jim Baughman, manager of corporate management development, who says, "Best practices has legitimized plagiarism."

But perhaps the most dramatic application of benchmarking occurred at GE's appliances plant in Louisville, Kentucky. On the basis of benchmarking inputs and the plant's own process mapping, Louisville has been able to speed its manufacturing rates and cut costs by keeping sufficient inventories of cheap components and developing just-in-time programs with the suppliers of the more expensive parts. The effect was to reduce inventory by $200 million, increase the return on assets (ROA) by 8.5 percent, and reduce the eighty-day cycle time by over 75 percent (Tichy and Sherman, 1993a). Louisville has become a major benchmarking stop for GE executives and for many benchmarking organizations around the world. Dennis Dammerman, GE's chief financial officer, says, "We must constantly evaluate our own performance and look for ways to make continuous improvement." He sees this as a business-by-business approach: "We have to map each process and benchmark the time required. That is, we have to compare cycle time to where we've been in the past, but we also have to compare ourselves to the best in the world" (Shah, 1991, pp. 413–414).

Concluding Thoughts

About now it would be fair for you to ask just how benchmarking is done. In Chapter One I'll answer this question, look at some of the process models that are available, and focus on a simple method that can be used to search for the best practices possible.

Part One

The Benchmarking Process

Chapter One

Doing It Right

The Models, Methods, and Processes
of Successful Benchmarking

> The more you learn, the more acutely aware you
> become of your ignorance. Thus, a corporation
> cannot be "excellent" in the sense of having
> arrived at a permanent excellence; it is always in
> the state of practicing the disciplines of learning, of
> becoming better or worse.
> —*Peter M. Senge,* The Fifth Discipline

An old Spanish proverb advises travelers to remember that "there are no roads. Roads are made by walking." Benchmarking is a journey in this proverb's sense because it is an evolving process and a learning experience. As you work with benchmarking and become comfortable using it, you will find that you can modify it to meet your organization's needs better. By observing what your competitors are doing and projecting their future performance you will learn how they operate, how their methods may make sense for your organization, and how you might adapt and build upon such practices. The more you benchmark, the more you will learn about the benchmarking process itself. Eventually you and your people will gain confidence in the process's ability to produce hard, reliable data—the kind of data upon which to plan and execute effective strategies to meet your customers' requirements. Ultimately, benchmarking will give you the kind of information you can use to attain leadership for your organization.

Benchmarking Methods

Many models and methods have been developed to explain and guide the benchmarking process. They range from a four-phase process used by DEC to a six-step process used by Alcoa to a nine-step model used by AT&T, with several others falling in between. All the models evolve from the original ten-step, four-phase model developed by Xerox and defined by Bob Camp. All the approaches are valid but no matter which is employed, a sound benchmarking program is always rooted in an iterative process that includes a minimum of four phases: establishing the study plan, conducting the study, diagnosing the data, and internalizing the results and taking action. (See Figure 1.1.)

Phase One: Establishing the Study Plan

When you establish the study plan, you take the steps to get ready to conduct a study. Several questions must be answered in order for a benchmarking plan to be established:

- What subject will be benchmarked?
- Which organizations should be benchmarked?

Figure 1.1. The Benchmarking Process.

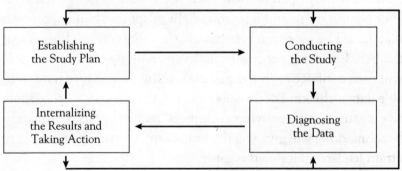

- What method or methods will be used to gather the data?
- Who will gather the data?

There are many opportunities to look at in deciding what to benchmark. First, what are your organization's—or your function's—deliverables, and how do you determine when you have been successful in meeting your goals? Second, what are the performance measures for your function and for the work processes within your function? These factors need to be taken into consideration when determining the appropriateness of subjects for study and the level of detail needed.

Once you have chosen some subjects for study, you will have to document the work processes involved. You need to do this both to understand the process fully and to help you make your final subject selection. A simple flowchart is the easiest way to accomplish both objectives.

Next, you will need to prepare a brief purpose statement for your study. It should discuss the subject, the measurements involved, and the ways in which the results will help you run your operations better. This purpose statement is like a mission statement: it will be a "touchstone" throughout the study, helping to assure that you stay on course.

A variety of sources are available to help you select partners for a benchmarking study. You can start by asking your organization's salespeople who they compete with in the marketplace. Ask your suppliers for the names of other customers. Information in the public domain may also provide many leads.

As noted in the introduction to this volume, internal benchmarking provides data that are certain to be highly relevant—and also relatively easy to collect—so in searching for potential benchmarking partners, it is smart to think about operations within your own organization first. Of course, direct competitors are logical partners, as are the leaders of generic functions (such as billing, payroll, and human resources). In fact, almost any organization or operation may possess information that can be used in a quest for improvement opportunities.

The next step in Phase One is to determine which kind of data will be collected. There are three basic sources of information: (1) internal sources, such as functional experts, marketing analysts, and company libraries; (2) information in the public domain, or secondary research, which can be gained through library searches, professional associations, consultants, and in external reports; and (3) original research, including that gained through questionnaires, telephone surveys, and personal visits. Usually all three sources are tapped in a benchmarking study, including some combination of the three methods of original research. Final selection of your plan will ultimately depend on the amount and accuracy of the data needed, the cost of obtaining that data, and the amount of time available and when you must have the results of the study.

At this point the people who will conduct the research must be chosen—yourself, someone in your department (or in another department), or a consultant. The task will probably require more than one individual (see Chapter Three for more on this). The structure of the benchmarking team will be determined based on the level of technical knowledge required and the scope of the study.

The last step in completing a benchmarking plan is to secure a "management champion" for the study. Some managers are likely to resist the idea of a benchmarking study, especially if they think the results will be threatening to them. Such resistance can be countered by gaining early buy-in among the managers who will be most affected by the results. Enlisting the personal support of either the senior manager responsible for taking action on the study's results or a peer manager will not only make communications and implementation easier—in essence, checkmating obstruction—but will also facilitate obtaining the resources and the time you'll need to conduct the study.

Establishing the study plan is discussed in depth in Chapter Two.

Phase Two: Conducting the Study

You must take three actions during Phase Two:

- Develop the questions you want answered.
- Finalize a plan for data collection.
- Implement your plan and collect the data.

The starting point for actually conducting a benchmarking study is to develop the list of questions you will ask your partners. The questions you choose will be based on the subject you wish to explore. You want to be certain that the questions are thorough but not overly burdensome. After you have developed a set of questions, go ahead and answer them yourself. This is a necessary step for three reasons. First, if your questions are too difficult for you to answer yourself, they will be too difficult for others. Second, you will ensure in this way that you have valid questions. Third, your own answers to your questions are essential to help you evaluate your partner's responses.

Next, you will have to finalize the method that is most appropriate for gathering the data. There are several things to consider in making this decision:

- The type and complexity of the information you want to gather
- The level of detail required and how the data will be used
- The time required by the method and the time actually available
- The resources required by the method and the resources actually available
- The experience level of the people conducting the study

All of these factors must be taken into consideration when you are deciding on which data collection method to use. Although a study can be conducted solely on the basis of one method, you are likely to use a combination, if not all four, of the methods available. The methods are *secondary research, surveys, telephone interviews,* and *personal visits*.

Secondary Research. Much of the information you want—perhaps all of it—is available in the public domain. From stockbroker analyses and government reports to annual reports and articles in periodicals, a vast array of sources will yield a vast amount of statistical and anecdotal information. At the very least, such research is essential in helping you choose the organizations that will make the best partners for your study and decide upon the questions you will ask (remember, benchmarking is an iterative process). However, it may yield all the information you require.

Mail Surveys. Mail surveys are perhaps the most commonly used method for gathering large amounts of data. They provide an easy means for partners to respond to specific questions and they are relatively inexpensive to use. Many benchmarking organizations begin their data gathering with surveys and use the findings to screen partners for follow-up questions and visits.

Telephone Surveys. Telephone interviews are extremely important, both as a means of following up on information acquired through secondary research or mail surveys and as a simple, convenient, and inexpensive means of gathering new data. Such interviews need to be structured—preferably through a questionnaire—to ensure that your partners' time is not wasted and that you acquire the information you need.

Personal Visits. Personal meetings with a partner's representatives and visits to observe a work site and work process are the most powerful experiences in benchmarking. A meeting with the people who actually conduct the work processes and influence the outcomes of those being benchmarked provides the opportunity to confirm your prior research, gather more data, and assess veracity and candor. It is important to note that not all visits to observe work processes or facilities require prior approval.

Your conduct during a site visit must be strictly professional. Ultimately, the benchmarking process depends on cooperation between people who adhere to the highest ethical standards. To assure that your efforts are successful and build relationships that will allow you to replicate your experience in the future, you will have to pay strict attention in several areas.

Be certain that your travel schedule allows you to arrive on time and to stay as long as needed to complete the visit. Discuss in advance the number of people who will make the visit with you. Submit in advance the questions that you want to ask. Bring your own data with you. If it is desirable to observe a work process, set up the tour beforehand. Never violate the law and always maintain the highest ethical standards.

Conducting the study is discussed in detail in Chapter Three.

Phase Three: Diagnosing the Data

Once the data have been obtained and you are back in your own office, the really difficult work of benchmarking begins. Beginning benchmarkers are often surprised to see how much data they have acquired during the research process. To avoid what is often described as "analysis paralysis" keep your purpose statement on hand as you begin to analyze the data you have gathered. Your objective is to satisfy the purpose statement and to answer four simple questions: Is one or more of your partners better than you are? If so, how much better? Why is it better? What have you learned or what can you learn from it?

Diagnosis—or analysis—of the data begins with pulling together all the data gathered and putting it into a form that allows for easy evaluation. The key is to keep it simple and to the point. The best way to determine if one of your partners is performing better than you are is to establish a simple matrix of the measures you have selected for evaluating the specific process you are bench-marking. What do the data say? Are the differences in performance measures clear? How large are the performance gaps? A perfor-mance gap thus becomes nothing more than the delta between your metric and your partner's metric. The results will indicate one of three types of performance gaps:

- *Negative*. A partner's practices are superior to your own.
- *Parity*. There is no appreciable difference between you and your partners.
- *Positive*. You are the benchmark with superior practices.

But you can't stop here. If the performance levels—the pro-ductivity rates—between your organizations are different, then over time the gap between you is likely either to widen or narrow. Thus you must project the gap over a reasonable time period—three to five years is typical. Doing this will help determine the kind of corrective action your organization will need to take.

The next step in analyzing the data is to determine *why* the benchmark organization is the leader. There may be several reasons why one organization is more effective than another and under-standing them will be important in determining what action plans you need to take. A variety of causes should be considered—busi-ness practices, work processes, performance standards, the local environment, local economics, and the organization's culture.

Chapter Four discusses in depth the data analysis process.

Phase Four: Internalizing the Results and Taking Action

The final phase in benchmarking is to communicate the findings, take corrective action, and monitor the implementation of the action plans.

In communicating the study's results it is necessary to engage the study's champion and all those people who are most affected by the results. But before the actual final communication can take place, the organization's current goals need to be reviewed to determine what changes will be necessary. When the communication takes place there should be unanimous support for your action plan. Finally, the monitoring of your action plan's implementation and progress needs to be built into all of your organization's vital business processes, such as planning and management processes. For example, any changes to your functional plans will also require adjustments to your strategic plans, and tactical action plans will necessitate adjustments to your current operating plan as well as the individual performance assessment plans of certain managers and employees.

The final step is to plan for follow-up studies in order to stay current with your partners, who are constantly improving. Such follow-ups will also help underscore the importance of benchmarking to the organization for target setting and pursuit of industry best practices.

This last phase of the benchmarking process is discussed in detail in Chapter Five.

Key Factors for Success

One way to make sure that you know how to do a benchmarking study is to understand what successful benchmarking really is. Certainly you will have succeeded if your study's objectives are met, but you will *know* you have succeeded when you recognize four aftereffects in your organization: a thorough understanding of the benchmarking process, management commitment to benchmarking, openness to change and a willingness to make changes in the organization's work processes, and implementation of action plans and follow-up studies.

A Thorough Understanding of the Benchmarking Process

In his book *The Benchmarking Workbook*, Greg Watson (1992) describes an experience he had while at Compaq. A Fortune 100 company that had just started to use benchmarking wanted to benchmark Compaq and Watson agreed to participate. He learned later that the company had selected Compaq as its only bench-marking partner and had submitted a questionnaire of fifty-seven questions that it wanted to have answered during a four-hour, face-to-face meeting. This procedure allowed only a four-minute response to each question and no time for discussion or follow-up. Watson contrasted this approach with that of Xerox, which wanted to benchmark Compaq on the same topic. Xerox submitted only eleven questions that would be discussed during a daylong session. The delta between these two examples is the result of benchmark-ing experience and the discipline that comes from following a stock process. When an organization follows a structured benchmarking process—one that their partner understands and can also follow—it is able to identify its needs more effectively and focus its efforts and resources. The result is a higher quality of information than would otherwise be acquired.

Along with an understanding of the benchmarking process, an organization must have a clear and comprehensive understanding of how its own work is conducted so that it can portray it in a way that its partners can both grasp and relate to. This kind of clarity is necessary in order to have a solid basis of comparison with the work practices of your benchmarking partners.

Management Commitment to Benchmarking

Benchmarking succeeds when senior management fully compre-hends the process and agrees to its use. Nothing can be more disas-trous to a benchmarking procedure than to gather data that suggest that one or more operations of your organization are being outper-formed by the competition without the commitment of some seg-ment of top management to act on this information. Without management commitment, benchmarking often brings out the ten-dency to defend oneself, producing a variety of emotional reactions and usually doing more harm than good. Indeed, management must not only support the benchmarking effort but also agree to consider the necessary changes. Of course, in order for change to be effective management will have to fund the changes and follow up during implementation. It is also important that top management not "punish" their organizations when they learn that others are performing better. Negative responses will work against the objectives of benchmarking, which are to find the best of class and motivate performance improvement.

Continuous improvement and the pursuit of best practices is a long-term commitment, and management must accept benchmarking as a primary means to accomplish these goals. Probably the single most important factor in managers' behavior is whether they are willing to learn from others, that is, from others inside the organization and outside it. The best benchmarking partners are those that are open, cooperative, willing to share, and, of course, best of class in the benchmark areas. It helps to "think outside the box"—to be open to nontraditional processes and solutions—because the best of class must be pursued no matter where it occurs.

Finally, management has to learn how to institutionalize benchmarking as a means of establishing goals and guiding strategic planning. Managers have to help the organization recognize that benchmarking partners do not stand still but are continuously improving. It is not enough just to get a snapshot picture and begin a plan of corrective action. The organization must continue to improve against a moving target. To accomplish this, senior management has to work continually at educating the organization first to focus on the best practice and then use metrics to understand the delta that needs to be overcome, rather than the other way around. Indeed, the most crucial indicator of success will always be the strong, concerted, and interested support of management.

Openness to Change and a Willingness to Change

Benchmarking has to be approached with an open mind. Successful practitioners of benchmarking always take an impartial, honest, and unassuming stance and are candid about the opportunities for improvement with the managers above and below themselves.

Open and honest evaluation of what the benchmarking data say is vital in order to make the best use of them. Such an evaluation will also help a company avoid benchmarking's greatest pitfall: comparing "apples" with "oranges." In a Conference Board survey (1993) on benchmarking, Pfizer reported miscommunication and misinterpretation of data as major concerns. For example, Pfizer discovered that different companies meant different things when they talked about *alignment*. For one company, alignment meant alignment with a division's business goals; for another it meant alignment of goals and strategies at the corporate level. Pfizer also found that surveys carried out by third parties did not relieve the likelihood of miscommunication and felt it was best to talk directly to the benchmarking partners.

The ultimate positive effect of openness is the organization's ability to change plans and goals in anticipation of a competitor's actions. You will know that you are successful when your organization is willing to share information with benchmarking partners and maintain a disciplined process for acquiring and using benchmarking data. Darrel Hull, manager of distribution planning for AT&T's material management services, says, "If benchmarking is to be effective, then there has to be an honest and free sharing of information" (Geber, 1990, p. 38). This is why senior management, when it recognizes the need for change and improvement, must repeatedly demonstrate that it is willing to make the tough decisions needed for success. Of course, the real test of openness is in how open the organization is to new ideas and change.

Implementation of Action Plans and Follow-Up Studies

Ultimately, the success of any benchmarking study depends upon the actions taken as a result of the study and the establishment of measures for tracking improvements. Managers facilitate change when they are involved and provide their personal support to those engaged in implementing change. Tichy and Sherman (1993a, p. 195) observe that as "speed, quality, and productivity become ever more important, corporations need people who can instinctively act the right way, without instructions, and who feel inspired to share their best ideas with their employees." Such behavior cannot be decreed or bought—rather, it has to be earned by managers who stand for the values that people in the organization want to believe in and then "act on those values, day in and day out." One way that Dave Kearns, Xerox's CEO at the launch of benchmarking, accomplished this was to demand that managers "expect what they inspect"—that is, learn to coach their employees by inspecting the steps used to accomplish the results—and demonstrate their involvement by "walking like you talk." When benchmarking studies are followed up with this kind of zeal, the benchmarking process is truly integrated into the management process.

Concluding Thoughts

In the experience of successful benchmarking organizations, once a work practice is understood and measured, management and the people who will have to implement the changes can get behind the new goals. These organizations know that employees are likely to support improvement efforts and be willing to change their operation's processes if they have reliable external information that compares them to an operation that is clearly a better performer. Armed with this kind of information, they will enthusiastically make any changes necessary. It is this kind of enthusiasm that leads to superior performance. How to create, harness, and support this kind of enthusiasm is what benchmarking is all about. In the next four chapters we explain how you do it.

Chapter Two

Phase One

Establishing the Study Plan

It is stupid to lose a game if it is possible to win by
being prepared.

—*Charles V. (Chuck) Mather,*
Winning High School Football

Any coach worth his salt would never allow his team to compete
without a game plan. Similarly, armies put hundreds of hours into
logistical and operational plans before a battle. In his biography,
General Norman H. Schwarzkopf (1992, pp. 288–289) described
the scope of the preparations for Desert Storm: "Each of the services had to flesh out its portion of the new war plan, and central
command had to assess the feasibility of delivering the necessary
forces and supplies to the war zone. Then a companion logistical
plan had to be prepared, consisting of thousands of pages of computer printouts that would specify how and in what order troops,
pieces of equipment, and supplies would actually be shipped. (Pen-
tagoners call this plan a 'topfiddle,' short for 'time-phased force
deployment list.') Normally a command could not adopt an operating plan until all of these time-consuming steps were completed."
As for managers, even one with minimal experience would hesitate
to direct staff to perform work without explaining what to do, how
to do it, and what resources to use. Thus, the coach, the general,
and the manager all have one thing in common: they want a plan
of action.

Purpose of Phase One

Most benchmarking projects start in one of two ways: a manager decides to try out this new tool or a senior manager requests that a benchmarking project be launched as quickly as possible. It may seem reasonable to embrace Nike's theme and "just do it" because it is what you want to do or because management wants it and it is prudent to do what management wants without hesitation. Yet it is always wise to avoid such knee-jerk reactions. As the saying goes, "Fools rush in where angels fear to tread."

Although it is wise to heed the requests of your management and to be sensitive to your organization's needs, it is equally wise to remember that benchmarking is a structured, methodical process and not a quick fix or a cure-all. Benchmarking requires thoughtful, deliberate integration of information on competitive process, practices, and performance measures into your goal-setting and decision-making processes. Unlike a reference book that allows you to look up the correct answer, benchmarking is a learning experience through which you improve your ability to gather the information that will help you set realistic performance goals based on the competitive environment. This is why benchmarking is often described as "evergreen." It offers a long life of continuous discovery in which you keep learning. It is an experiential process because before you can build the strategies that will lead to world-class performance you must understand how world-class organizations operate. Once you have this understanding, you will discover which of their practices your own organization can adapt. The organizations that use benchmarking this way are the ones that successfully establish priorities, targets, and practices that reach beyond their current practices. They stretch their expectations in delicate, measured ways that lead them to positions of competitive advantage in their markets.

To begin the planning phase it helps to acknowledge some simple but often overlooked facts about planning in general. First, any planning activity recognizes the needs of tomorrow because it is aimed at future accomplishments. In other words, at the same time that a plan is used to guide today's actions it is also used to cause a planned future to happen. Therefore, after all your work in Phase One is finished and you have a benchmarking plan laid out before you, you will possess not only a plan but also a clear idea of your direction and what you have to do to get there. The process is as important as the outcome. Also, the motivation of the participants will grow as they see feasible methods of getting what the organization wants. Everyone contributing to such a benchmarking study plan will be more focused. To the extent that they have helped develop the plan, they will be committed to its successful conclusion.

Of course, any planning process needs to be done with the knowledge that much of what is decided now will change as both the plan and the future unfold. In benchmarking, this is partly the result of the natural learning curve. But it is also a basic truism that when you build any plan your plan will cause you to become more alert to what is happening around you and, in turn, to adapt it to deal with actual events. Because of all the thinking you have done, you are more acutely aware of what is going on around you in the organization and see actions that affect the operations that you would not have noticed previously.

There are some dangers at this stage of the benchmarking planning process that have to be avoided. For one thing, once laid out, the task may turn out to be more imposing than you expected. When this happens it is easy to lose sight of your purpose by lowering expectations and aiming at lesser priorities—aspiring to less. Rather than allow this to happen, you must continue to believe that you will increase your chances of influencing the future if you focus on a few top priorities.

Types of Benchmarking Studies

One way to avoid these problems is to give serious consideration to the different types of benchmarking. As was discussed in the introduction to this volume, you can begin assembling the elements of your benchmarking plan by deciding on which of the three types of benchmarking studies will be most appropriate: internal studies, competitor studies, or functional (generic) studies.

1. *Internal studies*. Internal studies are relatively easy to conduct, usually cost less than studies of external competitors, offer a good learning experience, and can help define the scope of future studies.

2. *Competitor studies*. Studies of direct competitors are more readily accepted than internal studies, are widely accepted among organizations, and are likely to have a higher payback for the investment.

3. *Functional (generic) studies*. Functional competitors—or indus-try leaders in dissimilar industries—are usually not direct competitors and are therefore easier to approach than direct competitors. Yet such studies usually offer applicable lessons because generic processes performed by a wide cross section of firms are often easily transferable.

To decide which kind of benchmarking study is best for your organization, you will want to consider three other factors (Camp, 1989):

- *Relevance*. Are the data you will acquire likely to be applica-ble to your operations?
- *Ease of data collection*. How difficult will it be to uncover the data you will need?
- *Innovative practices*. Are you likely to discover an innovation that could lead to a breakthrough in either technology or your work process?

Table 2.1 shows how each study type stacks up. For example, when you benchmark an internal division or department it is rela-tively easy to acquire data; at the very least there should be no

Table 2.1. A Rating of Types of Benchmarking Studies.

Benchmarking Operation	Relevance	Ease of Data Collection	Innovative Practices
Internal operations	High	High	Low
Direct competitors	High	Low	Low
Functional (generic) processes	Low	High	High

reluctance to share data. Furthermore, you are certain to find information that will be compatible with your own operations. As Stephen McIntosh, Pittsburgh Plate Glass's director of training, says: "We have had much success in learning across businesses" (Marquardt and Reynolds, 1994, p. 221). However, the chances are you will not discover anything innovative because if a breakthrough had already occurred, it would most likely have been communicated to your division. When you benchmark a direct competitor, you can also expect that what you learn will be highly relevant to your business, but you will have more difficulty obtaining the data. You will also be equally unlikely to uncover an innovative practice.

As you start assembling the elements of your plan, be sure to keep in mind that the advantage benchmarking offers basically comes from two actions: uncovering the practices that are the foundation of the benchmark organization's performance and finding a way to transfer those benchmark practices to your organization. Because of the differences between internal and external environments, the benchmark practices of greatest benefit in other organizations may not always produce benchmark products or leadership processes. This is the reason that product and process benchmarking should not rest solely on performance metrics as the means for identifying best business practices.

It is also helpful to think about benchmarking studies in terms of their goals. This classification system gives us *performance benchmarking*, *strategic benchmarking*, and *process benchmarking*.

Performance Benchmarking

Performance benchmarking refers to any research that helps you assess your relationship with competitors and industry leaders in terms of price, product quality, product features (including service factors), or other performance measures. This is the kind of research that uses trend analysis from database searches or surveys. It requires the lowest investment because it can usually be accomplished through a review of public documents and can be carried out by an experienced research librarian or market research expert.

Strategic Benchmarking

Strategic benchmarking is a way to focus on the potential changes an organization can adapt by sharing data with noncompeting companies in order to identify significant business trend opportunities. Most commonly these studies are made by establishing benchmarking alliances with noncompeting organizations who then come together to share data and anecdotal information across a table. General Electric is probably the most successful proponent of this method. The investment is greater here than in performance benchmarking because strategic benchmarking requires a small team of professionals and long-term continuity. Compensation surveys, which have been carried out for years, are a good example of this method.

Process Benchmarking

Process benchmarking requires face-to-face studies and observations of a business's key processes, including customer billing, technology transfer, product delivery, and strategic planning. Because process benchmarking requires the participation of subject matter experts, the owner of a process and the process team (the people who actually do the work) should be directly involved in the study. This kind of research requires the greatest investment of labor and time.

Looking at benchmarking through these classifications enables an organization to build its benchmarking capabilities gradually. If you start with performance benchmarking, you can gradually increase your investment and build partnerships with a set of companies who understand the strategic issues for your company. Incidentally, some of the companies you solicit can include your suppliers and major customers. As Raymond Manganelli and Mark Klein point out in *The Reengineering Handbook* (1994, p. 122), often these companies "are also the customers and suppliers of other companies, sometimes of your competitors. Sometimes they have direct experience with the companies you are trying to benchmark." Once the strategic process is mastered you can go on to process benchmarking.

Objectives of Phase One

Once you have determined why your organization should use benchmarking and how benchmarking will help you improve your performance, you are ready to begin the first phase of the process—laying out the plan. In this part of Phase One the basic elements that make up any benchmarking plan must be developed. These elements are choosing a benchmarking subject, determining the best measurement, documenting the work process, writing a purpose statement, selecting the best organizations as your partners, choosing the best way to gather the data, and developing a questionnaire.

The overall aim is to *organize*, that is, to ensure that the project has a clear focus by prioritizing the functions or processes to study, selecting benchmarking partners, obtaining support from process "owners" and stakeholders, and assigning the project to a team. A benchmarking team usually has from three to eight members, including representatives from all the functions that manage the process under study. (We'll say more about this in the next chapter.) The team's responsibility is to prepare a project plan, with input from the people involved in the process, that outlines the scope and purpose, proposed benchmark measures, methodology, and resources needed (Bogan and English, 1994).

The balance of this chapter examines in detail the steps to be taken in Phase One.

Choosing a Benchmarking Subject

Too many organizations do not take the time to focus their efforts properly when deciding what to benchmark. They believe that a "silver bullet" is waiting to be found, but they wait in vain. The truth is that each step of each phase of the benchmarking process requires painstaking attention to detail, beginning with the decision of what to benchmark.

This decision requires consideration of many things. Perhaps the most obvious is your own organization's deliverables or outputs and how you measure if the outputs are achieved. Also, what specific performance measures are used for your function and for its work processes? All of these criteria and more have to be considered in order to identify the appropriateness of the outputs you want to study and the level of detail you will need.

To select what will be benchmarked you must always focus on a work process. Which of the work processes in your organization are the most critical to its overall success? Examples of work processes that can be benchmarked are technology delivery, time to market, unit manufacturing costs, customer delivery process, and product quality.

Another approach is to look at the outputs of your work processes. Since every function of an organization delivers a product, at least in the broad sense of the term (a service call, a financial report, or an actual product your external customers purchase), benchmarking is equally applicable to all products.

Begin by reviewing your organization's mission statement, goals, and objectives. Then ask yourself some questions. For example, given its goals, which of your work processes are the most critical to the overall success of your operation? What products or services do you provide? Without the answers to these questions you will find it difficult to winnow out the most important processes. Because there are so many things to evaluate during a search for the right benchmarking subjects, it is best to develop a list of choices. Make an inventory of subjects, basing it on three factors: your organization's critical success factors, customer satisfaction, and cost of quality.

Critical Success Factors

Every organization has a mission statement or some other explanation of its strategy. Such statements of purpose are supported by a set of primary objectives, which are usually broken down into the specific actions or targets that are most responsible for achieving the objective. Contained within these actions and targets are the key events that must occur in order for the process to produce the objective successfully. Such "key events" are often called critical success factors (CSFs). Benchmarking CSFs can help an organization gain insight into actions that have a direct impact on their objectives. Spendolini (1992) points out that rather than seeking competitive data based on measurements you have established, it is much more effective to begin with a specific CSF and then expand your inquiry to the broader process issues. Spendolini classifies CSFs on three levels:

Level 1. A level-1 CSF defines a broad subject area for investigation, possibly involving an organizational department or function that is usually too broad to involve any type of measurement. Examples are billing, the procurement process, corrective action procedures, customer satisfaction levels, marketing and promotions.

Level 2. A level-2 CSF defines a more specific area of investigation than a level-1 CSF. A level-2 CSF can often be defined by some type of aggregate measure, such as the number of customer complaints, the number of promotions per time period, average salary levels, and overall number of billing errors.

Level 3. A level-3 CSF is the most specific level that can be defined, particularly by means of some type of measure or specific process description that allows your benchmark partner to produce information comparable to your own. Examples are annual budget for television, advertising by market, processes for reducing scrap rates by product line, and methods for determining bad debt expenses as a percent of sales.

Fitz-enz (1993) suggests that organizations look at CSFs to consider how improving them would affect market share. He suggests six questions to help identify the key CSFs within departments:

1. What is the highest value-potential factor in our function? That is, what outcome would most help our organization achieve its mission?
2. Is the greatest value to be found in improving quality, productivity, or service?
3. Which processes are most critical in achieving that value?
4. Which processes currently show the greatest room for improvement?
5. Which processes might be easiest to fix?
6. Will the final competitive advantage for the company come from an increase in revenue, a reduction in operating expense, or an improvement in customer satisfaction?

Asking several other questions may also help you make the final selection of a CSF:

1. Is the CSF quantifiable? If so, how? Is it measurable? If so, how?
2. Can the CSF be audited? If so, how and where?
3. Over time does this CSF show process results and progress toward a key goal?

4. Is this measure accepted by other organizations? Is it accepted within your own organization?

5. Are the data easy or difficult to obtain?

Customer Satisfaction

The phrase "The customer is always right" is no longer a cliché because achieving customer satisfaction is what separates the winners from the losers in today's global economy. Phil Crosby (1992, p. 229), a noted quality consultant, describes satisfied customers as "successful customers" and succinctly underscores the importance of customer satisfaction by saying: "The key to having a successful customer is in determining what that customer wants and then arranging the operation to produce that."

When you review your organization's customer satisfaction activities for possible benchmarking subjects, ask yourself these questions: What are the key factors in the organization for achieving customer satisfaction? How is customer satisfaction measured? The actual measure used to gauge customer satisfaction with your products and services will, of course, depend on your business and your products. But such metrics exist whether you use them today or not. For example, one steel company (we'll call it ABC Steel) used customer satisfaction to choose a subject for its benchmarking study. ABC needed to improve its unit manufacturing costs. Although its product durability and strength was equal to or better than its competitors, its overall manufacturing costs were high. The company selected the CSFs it wanted to benchmark after analyzing all of the processes that affected its manufacturing costs:

- Maintaining excellent supplier relationships
- Achieving customer satisfaction
- Merchandising available inventory to its most value-added use
- Utilizing available capital and human resources effectively

ABC judged that customer satisfaction was the most critical of its CSFs and decided that that was where it wanted to make its benchmarking investments. The following list shows the specific benchmarking metrics that ABC selected to measure the effectiveness of its customer relations CSF.

- Sales per customer
- Order to bid ratio
- Number of complaints
- Number of inquiries
- Number of new accounts
- Percent of on-time deliveries
- Number of late payments
- Tone of ABC's telephone operator's voice

Cost of Quality

The cost of quality measurement was developed by Crosby (1979) and represents a dramatic way to help people in continuous quality improvement. To put it briefly, cost of quality is the cost of nonconformance to customer requirements plus the cost of conforming to customer requirements. This aggregate cost of quality can be used to create awareness, prioritize opportunities, and broadly assess progress in all functions and operations. Crosby estimates that large companies spend 15 to 20 percent of their sales on nonconformance alone. Capturing even a small amount of these nonconformance costs would have a profound effect on any organization's bottom line. There are six elements to the cost of quality (Schmidt and Finnigan, 1992, p. 208):

1. *Cost of prevention* refers to the cost of up-front activities to prevent failure from happening. Examples are training and capital expenditures.

2. *Cost of appraisal* refers to the costs incurred to determine conformance with quality standards. Inspection and auditing are the most common examples.

3. *Cost of internal failure* refers to the costs of correcting products or services that do not meet quality standards prior to delivery to a customer, such as engineering design changes and invoice errors.

4. *Cost of external failure* refers to the costs incurred to correct products or services after delivery to the customer. Field retrofits, sales commission adjustments, and service expenses fall into this category.

5. *Cost of exceeding requirements* are costs incurred to provide information or services that are unnecessary or unimportant to the customer (or for which no known requirement has been established). Unread reports, product features a customer does not use, or sales calls with no purpose are common examples.

6. *Cost of lost opportunity* refers to lost revenues that can result from customers choosing competitive products or services and from cancellations when products and services do not meet their requirements. Many organizations would argue that lost opportunity is impossible to measure; however, most sales representatives are usually able to figure out why they lose to competitors. In addition, incremental incentives, such as the automotive industry's cost of rebates, would be counted here.

Table 2.2 shows how an organization used cost of quality as a tool to identify functions or processes for benchmarking. In this example, most people would likely choose to benchmark "receiving and test" because the nonconformance costs are so large. Most people would also look for benchmark subjects in "assembly" because the conformance costs are dominant and in "shipping" because the conformance costs are so much greater than the nonconformance costs.

In addition to considering CSFs, customer satisfaction, and cost of quality, here are some other pertinent questions to ask when you

Table 2.2. A Cost-of-Quality Measurement.

Process	Conformance ($ million)	Non-conformance ($ million)	Total ($ million)
Receiving	2	6	8
Assembly	10	1	11
Test	5	4	9
Shipping	5	1	3
Accounting	2	1	8

are deciding on a subject for your study: What critical decisions does the organization have to make? Where is its competitive pressure coming from? What process measurements does it normally track? What subjects have already been benchmarked by the organization?

Once you have done all of this you should find you have a list of fertile subjects (for example, time to market, market share, unit manufacturing costs, product delivery process, and product quality). But before you lock in your final decision, it is wise to apply one final test. Ask these questions: How important is this subject to our supplier-customer chain? How important is this subject to the work process we are evaluating? Is there someone in management who agrees that this is important and will support implementing changes in the organization based on the study results; in other words, is there a champion for this benchmarking study at the next level of management?

Common Pitfalls

The experience of many organizations in selecting subjects shows that there are some common traps that newcomers to benchmarking should try to avoid. The first and most obvious is selecting a subject that is unimportant. Another is choosing too many subjects to study. Focusing on too many metrics is also a common error, as is picking metrics that don't provide meaningful data. But perhaps the two most harmful and commonly made mistakes for beginners are failing to define clearly the purpose of the study and failing to obtain management buy-in for the study, the subject, or the metrics. We'll talk more specifically about how to obtain management buy-in at the end of this chapter.

Once you have made your decision and locked into a subject you want to study, you are ready for the next step.

Selecting the Best Measurement

Almost everything we do in our lives can be measured against some standard—from how quickly we accomplish the major tasks of our job to how effectively we invest our savings. We can measure our own and our family's vacation "pleasure index" by evaluating this year's vacation against last year's or by comparing our vacation stories with Cousin Jack's. The truth is that anything can be measured once a proper metric is chosen. Choosing the proper metric is the next step in the benchmarking process.

Choosing a measure will not only provide the metrics for performance comparison with your partners but will also help to define the benchmarking subject itself. Let's say you choose "product quality" for your subject. What exactly will you measure? Reliability? Mean time to repair? Actual repair costs? All of these are important but each relates to a different aspect of product quality. Which is the more significant for your organization? Revisiting your list of CSFs may help you decide. Exhibit 2.1 shows some of the metrics commonly used in benchmarking. It is certainly not an all-inclusive list, but it will give you some idea of the kind of measurements that organizations use.

In *Benchmarking for Best Practices*, Christopher Bogan and Michael English (1994, p. 41) wrote that "successful best practice improvement strategies marry the study of metrics and processes" and they observed further that the "hallmark of a well-designed set of project benchmarks is that they enable measurement and comparisons across systems."

Exhibit 2.1. Examples of Benchmarking Metrics.

Cost and Cost-Related Metrics

- Share of cost of function revenue (percent)
  - Sales
  - Service
  - Customer administration
  - Distribution
  - General and administration
- Labor overhead rate (percent)
- Material overhead (percent)
- Manpower performance ratio
- Months of supply
- Cost per page of publication
- Cost per order
- Cost per engineering drawing
- Cost per line of programmed code
- Occupancy costs as percent of revenue
- Return on assets

Quality

- Percentage of parts meeting requirements
- Percentage of finished product quality improvement
- Number of problem-free products
- Internal and external customer satisfaction measures
- Billing error rate

Service

- Work support ratio
- Cost per Standard Available Call Activity Time (SACAT) hour
- Service response time
- First-time fix of service call problem
- Percentage of supplies delivered next day or on time
- Percentage of parts available for the service representative

It is also very important to select measurements that are true indicators of performance. Camp (1989, p. 51) advises that measurements should cover "unit cost, customer satisfaction level, and appropriate asset measurements." For example, in examining the effectiveness of a sales force, evaluation of the number of sales calls per day will be far more revealing than a comparison of the number of sales reps. Similarly, when considering cost controls for facilities, occupancy cost per square foot expense is more significant than square feet alone.

When one is working with numbers it is also a good idea to be cautious. Although numbers can impress, they usually say little about the underlying opportunities or dangers they represent. Therefore, in considering the appropriateness of a metric you should consider the following: How do you measure your own performance? Are there current internal measurements available, and if not, can they be calculated? Can other organizations be compared against your internal measurements on an "apples to apples" basis? Have you studied your own operations and methods well enough to know how this performance is achieved?

Documenting the Work Process

Once you know what you want to benchmark and how you are going to measure it, you will need to document the work process itself. For example, if you are going to benchmark product quality on the basis of reliability measures, how are the product reliability goals or measures achieved? That is, what work process or processes produce the result? Documenting a work process is best done by a detailed flowchart that reflects all the process steps—inputs and outputs—as well as the measures for each step. Such a flowchart would portray the input and output of the overall process and the input and output of each process step by showing the practices used and defining each of the critical measurements used. When the flowchart is complete, analyze the interrelationship of the steps for appropriate points of measurement and gain agreement from those who perform the work that the metrics really are the true indicators of the process performance—that is, unit cost, customer satisfaction levels, or asset measurements. Documenting the work process to be benchmarked in this manner will not only help you understand the process itself better but will also serve to double-check that you have chosen the right subject to benchmark.

There are other advantages to documenting the work process. The most important is to be certain that you understand it well enough to know what has to be measured and what can and cannot be studied. The second is to have a document to share with your benchmarking partners to be certain that you are comparing the same information about the same or similar processes. In other words, you can compare your flowchart with your benchmarking partners to be certain that you perform the same steps. You might find that your partner became the best of the best merely by removing unnecessary steps from its work process. Finally, you can use the flowchart to look for immediate improvements by considering the opportunities for cycle time reduction.

Writing a Purpose Statement

The next step is to put the purpose of your study into a statement. Such a narrative is the touchstone that you will use to make sure your work remains on target, representing a sort of mission statement for the study. Spendolini (1992, p. 68) uses the term *diagnostic summary* instead of purpose statement. He describes it as "simply a review of the issues that were discussed with the benchmark customers and a statement of the agreed-upon parameters that will guide the benchmarking investigation."

Your purpose statement should include the work processors' output and identify the customer for the study. It is a brief statement of the purpose of the project, the subject of the study, and the measurements involved. It should also indicate how the findings will help you run your business. For example, a purpose statement might read as follows: "The purpose of this study is to evaluate our current level of customer service compared to others as measured by mean time between failures. The results of this study will help service management determine if we are adequately staffed with service reps or if we can improve productivity by acquiring new test equipment." Such a statement is infinitely more helpful than this one: "The purpose of the study is to measure quality."

Selecting the Best Partners

Perhaps the most important decision of the planning phase is who will be your benchmarking partners. Choosing your partners is at least as important as choosing a subject because the data you acquire will have a long-term effect on your operations. Plan on carrying out careful research during the partner selection process. The easiest way to start is by compiling a list of external organizations or internal functions that might make good partners. Begin with a list of organizations that you consider to be either the industry leaders or your competitors. Next, add organizations that have good reputations—the organizations that you most admire. To develop this list you will want to consult the following resources: your customers; people in your department and those in other departments who perform similar functions; members of your professional or trade association; trade journals; reports from securities analysts and other financial reports; patent lists and business directories.

Jeff Miller says that many people make the mistake of only going after companies that have notoriety, such as those who win the Malcolm Baldrige National Quality Award. He points out that there are some innovative practices going on in companies that are struggling to get back on their feet. "People tend to neglect these companies because they aren't doing well. But you might find that they are doing some innovative things because their backs are to the wall. Look at the good companies, but don't neglect some less popular ones that may be doing some exciting things" (American Society for Training and Development, 1992, p. 2). Miller points to Xerox as an example. When struggling to survive in the early 1980s, its market share plummeted as a result of Japanese competition. "Nobody paid attention to them because they were struggling, yet they were perfecting this marvelous system we are calling benchmarking" (p. 2).

Although your major business competitors will probably be your first choices, you can also benchmark against other organizations that set functional standards. For instance, in addition to benchmarking its operations against IBM and Kodak, with whom they compete directly, Xerox also benchmarked against L. L. Bean, the leading mail order distributor of recreational clothing, because Bean is known for effective and efficient warehousing and distribution of its products. Think of "competitor" in the broadest sense. Ask yourself what organizations have the best functional or industry practices, and look for comparable operations where the best practices, methods, or processes are used, regardless of the business or operating purpose.

Looking for Comparable Partners

In looking for partners you will want to be certain that you have comparability. For example, if your organization values high customer satisfaction then only look for partners that share your values. If your business requires quick customer response time and turnaround, you will want to look at organizations that have the same respect for time. For example, Motorola studied Domino's Pizza and Federal Express to speed its delivery process. Finally, consider where the breakthroughs in business practices are usually found or likely to occur next.

Certainly, your competitors will come readily to mind, but it is a good idea to ask your customers who they think their up-and-coming suppliers are. And, of course, your own suppliers can tell you something about their customers. In addition, it is possible that one or more of the companies you'd consider benchmark companies *are* your major customers. If this is the case, consider the dual opportunity of learning from them while at the same time improving your relationship with them by demonstrating an interest in their processes or practices with the intent to improve your service to them.

Choosing Partners

From your list of potential benchmarking partners you will have to choose the final partners. First you will want to do some secondary research to boil the candidate list down to two or three organizations. A variety of sources can help you in this task, beginning with your salespeople, who compete with the marketplace leaders, and your suppliers, who have other customers in your field besides you. Go on to gather some information in the public domain on your potential partners. Then build a simple matrix that compares your measures with theirs. Of course, before you make your final decision you will want to be certain about the reliability of the information in your matrix. You might need to know if these companies really are in a business similar to yours or if there are differences between you that may invalidate the results of a study. Watson (1992) reviewed the literature on one company included in such a list and discovered in an obscure article written by one of that company's engineers that it had managed to integrate structured analysis methods with quality function deployment to specify software requirements. That information propelled the company to the head of his list.

Also consider if these organizations are friendly or unfriendly; that is, will obtaining data be more difficult than it is worth? And, once again, are you comparing apples to apples? For example, if the subject of the study is financial performance as measured by ROA and you have a mature business, you might want to eliminate small, fast-growing companies from your list because they generally have different cost structures. Camp (1989, p. 60) advises giving some consideration to a potential partner's structure: "Adjustments can be made during the analysis to ensure comparability, but the most value will be derived from similarly structured firms and operations."

Leila Kight, president of Washington Researchers LTD agrees that a company should not be excluded just because it isn't on top (American Society for Training and Development, 1992, p. 2): "You obviously want to choose companies that are good at those things you need to be better at. A misconception is that you have to benchmark against the best in the world. But anyone who is considerably better will have something to teach you. Also, you may never discover some techniques from the best in the world because they don't share information."

Making the Final Selection

The key factor in your final selection should be performance leadership, not accessibility. Xerox takes the process of choosing a company seriously. Careful research is the key. First, the benchmarking team puts together a candidate list based on the team's understanding of what it wants to benchmark. The team members do secondary research to boil the candidate list down to from three to six companies and then do extensive background checks on these companies before they even make contact. According to Camp (American Society for Training and Development, 1992, p. 2), Xerox looks at anything that is relevant in the company's last three to five years. "We look at anything that is in the public domain. We look for anything—from business information services, such as Dunn and Bradstreet, to annual reports to whatever is in the public press."

Michael Spendolini and Neil Thompson (1992) surveyed several benchmarking organizations and asked them why they screened out potential partners. (They called potential partners "suitors.") For one thing, they learned that too often potential partners have insufficient knowledge of their own process (and problems), which makes any comparisons meaningless to both parties. They also found that in many instances the suitors are insensitive to—or absolutely unaware of—the time demands their request would impose upon their partners.

Fitz-enz (1993) recommends three additional criteria in making partner selections: diversity, creativity, and desire. By diversity, he means having a representation of organizations from different types of business, size, and geography. By creativity, he means looking for innovation, no matter how wild the idea. An "off-the-wall" approach just might lead to a breakthrough where you would least expect it. Finally, he suggests observing those who have the desire to achieve leadership, organizations whose behavior (not necessarily their numbers) tell you at the gut level that they are striving for excellence and will probably make it.

Deciding to Be a Partner

Another company may ask you to be a partner in a benchmarking study. How do you make that decision? First, make the same kind of analysis you would if you were initiating the contact, then apply the following additional standards in order to determine if it will be a productive engagement for you:

1.   Has the host organization sufficient resources for the study? You want to avoid spending your resources on a study that will not be completed because the initiator has underestimated the required investment. Be especially certain of the availability of benchmarking resources in the functional areas to be studied at the host organization.

2.   Has the host organization made the adequate advance preparation? Does it have a specific benchmarking model in mind to follow; if so, how familiar is it with how the model works? Check if the host has charted the existing process to be benchmarked and reviewed literature about the process and potential partners. What is the extent of knowledge it has acquired about your organization and especially how the functional area to be studied operates in your organization?

3.   How committed is the host organization to the study? How much expertise does the host team's leader possess? Does its team have the backing of senior management and does the team include members of the function to be studied?

4.   Does the host team embrace a code of conduct? It is important that you both know which matters can be discussed and which are off-limits and you want to be certain that your host has considered these issues in an ethical context.

At Hewlett-Packard (HP) the process for determining whether a benchmarking engagement is appropriate calls for the requesting organization to submit six items in writing:

1. A copy of its questionnaire
2. Its statement of objectives (purpose of the study)
3. A list of the benefits for participating
4. Its rationale for picking HP (something more than "HP is a benchmark")
5. Evidence of current process documentation
6. Current process metrics or measures

The request is summarized by HP's benchmarking program manager and distributed to the appropriate units. All responses are returned to the requesting organization and if favorable, direct contact is made between the requestor and the functional HP person.

Common Pitfalls

The most common miscues at this stage of the process are not considering other units in one's own organization as potential partners, failing to consult with customers, and avoiding industry leaders because of the assumption that they will not want to reveal their secrets. Other mistakes include not using the public sources that are available for screening potential partners or for basic research, presuming that benchmarking applies only to corporate behemoths (when in fact small organizations can benchmark successfully if projects are scaled down and costs are contained), and failing to obtain management's buy-in to the partners to be benchmarked.

Determining the Best Way to Gather the Data

The next two planning steps are best done simultaneously and serve as a bridge between Phase One and Phase Two. The steps are determining how you will gather the data and deciding who will collect them. Phase Two begins with finalizing who will actually collect the data, and this decision is largely dependent on the collection method you select, as it is hard to separate them. Although we will cover deciding who will collect the data at the start of Chapter Three, in actual practice you will find that it helps to keep that subject in mind as you determine how you will gather the data. Of course, these decisions will be partly influenced by the type of study, that is, internal, competitive, or functional. But regardless of the type, before you can choose a method for data collection or select a person or persons to do the collecting, you will have to take into account the amount and accuracy of the data you will require, the cost of the study, and the time available to conduct the study.

Each of these factors will affect your study plan. For example, studying management development tracking systems requires a specific kind of expertise, probably does not necessitate the cost of a site visit, and because it is not usually a proprietary subject allows easy exchange of information. However, assessing the use of software design tools means probing into a totally different level of strategic sensitivity and entering a study that will certainly require investments in time and money as well as special software and design skills.

There are many sources of information available, but it is probably easiest to think in terms of two basic sources: internal sources, such as functional experts, marketing analysts, and your organization's libraries, and external information, such as public library searches, external reports, professional associations, consultants, and original research. Original research encompasses mail questionnaires, telephone surveys, and personal visits. In fact, many studies will require that both internal and external sources be used, including some combination of the three methods of original research. The following sources are the most commonly used:

- External reports, including financial reports, professional publications, trade journals, magazine articles, market research results, government data, library materials, and media reports
- Professional and trade associations, trade shows
- People in other units of the organization, corporate staff, quality specialists, and former employees of competitors; contact with your salespeople and your suppliers
- Consultant studies and industry experts
- Competitive product analysis
- Customer feedback
- Telephone and mail surveys
- Company visits

As already noted, your final choices will be influenced by considerations of the amount and accuracy of the data required, the costs of obtaining the data, and the time required to complete the study. You can zero in on an approach by starting with questions like the following: Do any of my employees have either direct contact with a competitor or know someone who might have information to share? If the information is difficult to obtain through a direct contact, would a third-party approach, where the results would be handled confidentially, be appropriate? How creative is our approach?

This last question is very important because in developing solutions to any difficulties you may have with resources and investments, the best advice is, Be creative! For example, some organizations have utilized graduate schools of business for their benchmarking studies. The results of these arrangements were valuable for the organizations' managers and excellent business experience for the students.

Data Sources

Although we will review the details of gathering data in the next chapter, before thinking about who will gather the data, it is helpful to think about the research methods available. As you consider which is best for your study, decide too what kind of specialists you need, such as electrical engineers or materials experts, to conduct or participate in the study. Keep in mind that it is wise to enlist the people with special interest or expertise in the subject to join you on the study team. Ideally, a benchmarking team is made up of the people who will have to implement any process changes.

There are several methods for data gathering. The task is to pick that method or combination of methods that will best meet your needs. Sources of competitive data available to you are limited only by your imagination and creativity. They might include your own personal and professional contacts, trade associations, technical journals, or advertisements. You can solicit information directly from a competitor or analyze its products.

Internal Information. Gathering data from internal sources is relatively easy to do, generally costs less than external efforts, offers a good learning experience, and can help define the scope of future external studies. In assessing the value of an internally based study there are three activities to consider: product analysis by reverse engineering and process reconstruction; company sources such as market research and functional experts, as well as recent hires; piggybacking with other studies already under way.

Reverse engineering is an expression that describes the process of disassembling a competitive product in order to evaluate its components and capabilities and probable manufacturing sequence and process. It is a traditional method through which manufacturing organizations assess their competitors' products. This same mentality can be applied when examining another organization's work process. If the literature provides you a description (or flowchart) of a work process, by the application of logic and collective assessment, you can often step back through the process to reconstruct its main elements.

Most organizations employ market research groups and industry analysts who regularly evaluate competitors and competitive activities. Much of the information that these specialists either have or can acquire can be helpful in assessing the key processes of organizations, such as time to market and product delivery. Although reconfiguring their evaluation processes or reexamining the data they possess may represent extra work for these specialists, whatever you have to do to tap into this source will be well worth the effort.

Common Pitfalls.   One pitfall to avoid is reinventing the wheel. It is not uncommon in large organizations for data gathering efforts to be duplicated. For this reason you will want to be certain that there is no study already under way that will produce the information you are seeking. If you discover that another function in your organization is already conducting a similar internal (or external) study, you may be able to piggyback, that is, add your additional requirements to it with minimal investments.

External Information.   Literature searches and other secondary research of published material, including corporate materials, are intended to obtain information of direct relevance and produce leads to other sources of information. Such materials range from annual reports to local newspaper articles, from papers presented at technical conferences to articles by vendors on product performance, and from reports by investment analysts to advertisements in trade publications.

Original research reaches past this to include some kinds of surveys, interviews, or face-to-face visits. In fact it includes a variety of single processes or combinations, such as mail survey or telephone interview, mail survey and telephone interview follow-up, telephone interview and mail survey follow-up, site visit and interview, site visit and telephone interview follow-up.

On-site visits—those done in order to study manufacturing operations, for example—may be critical. But when they involve your competitors, such visits may be difficult to arrange. In these cases you might want to consider trying to arrange for on-site visits by qualified observers not associated with your company. To make such visits cost-effective, attempt this only after you have determined that the target company and site are likely to provide information of significance to your assignment (McConagle, 1992).

The method you finally choose will depend on the complexity of the subject being benchmarked, the amount of time and budget you have, the people who will participate and their skills, and the willingness of the partners to make themselves (and their facilities) available.

The organizations with which I am familiar started benchmarking primarily by reading trade journals, corporate reports, and other public information about their competitors. This yielded mostly general information but also helped them crystalize the specifics they wanted to zero in on. As their data needs became more specific they adapted more specific approaches. A customer administration function, for example, decided it needed benchmarking data by which to assess and improve its own performance in customer support activities. After some initial data gathering, the team recognized the size and complexity of the undertaking. (Customer support activities have widely differing organizational structures from company to company.) They decided, therefore, to enlist a consultant to help design and conduct a survey to gather the needed information. This proved the most efficient and economic approach.

Developing a Questionnaire

Before deciding who should gather the data, you will need to clarify what information is to be gathered. Therefore, the next action to take is to develop a questionnaire—a list of the questions you want to have answered. A questionnaire is important because it documents all the questions of interest that you might have and helps outline all the data that can be gathered over an extended period of time. It allows for more extensive data gathering because it can be used in a number of settings—as a survey, as a guide for a telephone interview, and as a structure for information gathering during a site visit. The questionnaire will be your research guide during the project, regardless of whether you are doing an internal or external study.

Questionnaires should contain questions that cover at a minimum these two major areas:

1. *Best practices*. You will want to uncover everything you can about the your partners' work practices in order to uncover the best practices they maintain to achieve their planned outputs.
2. *Metrics*. In order to understand fully your partners' best practices you will need to identify the output ratios that support the best practices.

Some Guidelines

It is important to remember two things when you are developing your questionnaire. First, remember Greg Watson's story about Compaq's benchmarking study—the questionnaire should be short and specific. Second, make sure you can answer your own questions. By answering your own questions you may discover that the data are not as easy to obtain as you thought. Put succinctly, if you can't answer your questions, you can't expect anyone else to. Fitz-enz (1993) recommends asking the people in your organization most familiar with the subject to review the questionnaire and to make notes for you regarding any problems, also noting how long it took them to answer each question. He also asks that his evaluators comment on "which questions would have required them to go into the records to gather data that were not readily available" (p. 108).

There is another important reason for the questionnaire. You will need your own answers to the questions as a base point to compare the results from your partners. Of course, you will also need to provide your partners your own answers to these questions. As Watson (1992, p. 70) observes, "The comfort level of sharing the benchmark subject for both parties needs to be established." By having someone (preferably the people who manage, support, and use this particular work process in your organization) complete your questionnaire you will be able to address both issues. Certainly, the people who manage this process will not hesitate to point out the accuracy of your questions and assess the ease or difficulty of obtaining the data. Your purpose statement will also help focus the questionnaire appropriately.

The following guidelines will help you develop your questionnaire:

1. Review the purpose, subject, and measurements for the study.

2. Make sure the questions are clear. (Provide definitions, particularly for measurements.)

3. Use terms that are generally understood in your industry. A good rule of thumb is to avoid company jargon, but if it will clarify an issue, use industry jargon.

4. Make sure each question has a purpose and that the information obtained is relevant to the study.

5. Have the people who do the actual work critique and complete the questionnaire.

Specifics

Each question should specify the data you are looking for while at the same time clarifying the subject. For example, if you were probing into an organization's quality levels, you could ask: "What is your quality level?" Obviously, such a question leaves a lot open to interpretation and increases the control level of the person answering the question. Instead, you might ask for the same information this way: "In our company we measure quality by calculating service response time. Do you use a similar measurement technique? If your answer is yes, what has been your performance this year? If no, what measurement system do you use?" The second approach is more comprehensive because it provides an example, anticipates the effect of a forced-choice response (yes or no), and offers an open-ended alternative. The kinds of questions you ask will have a real effect on the kind of responses you receive.

Developing questionnaires is a science that most of us don't have the skills for. For this reason it is best to have some professional guidance. If you are in a large organization you might find you are fortunate enough to have psychometric experts available to you in your organizational development or employee research groups. Also, most market research functions either have this skill on their staff or know how to access it. If you haven't such internal resources, consider turning to a local university. Graduate students in organizational research, education, marketing, and operations research might be available to provide assistance as a graduate project or a part-time job.

Four types of questions can be used on a questionnaire. Each type yields a different kind of response:

- *Multiple choice*. For example, How do you select your systems: cost, support, or reputation?
- *Scaled*. For example, How important is cost in selecting systems: very important, important, somewhat important, not important?

- *Forced-choice*. For example, Do you consider cost when you select systems: yes or no?
- *Open-ended*. For example, How do you select systems?

Sharing

Successful benchmarking is dependent upon mutual exchange, and partners should be selected and agendas designed to ensure equal time for learning. Therefore, before you arrive at your partner's doorstep you have to think through what information you are willing to share. Miller (American Society for Training and Development, 1992, p. 2) says that there is an unwritten benchmarking code of conduct that states if you ask questions, expect to answer some yourself. Because benchmarking extends beyond competitive analysis, you really can't expect a company to reveal its secrets unless you are willing to do the same. In fact, you might think of benchmarking as the corporate equivalent of "I'll show you mine if you show me yours." Therefore, before you can implement your study plan you will have to decide what you can and cannot share and conduct your benchmarking study accordingly. Remember that competitors are often willing and eager to share information but only on a quid pro quo basis. In one such agreement the results of a customer administration study were provided to all partners in exchange for their participation. Recognizing the value of the data, one partner offered to help fund the follow-up study.

This is a good place to make an important point about benchmarking. Effective benchmarking requires the careful building of an environment of trust that is based on cooperation and learning between organizations. Developing this kind of trust requires more than a common process: it requires a shared understanding of ethical guidelines. Although we'll cover this in more detail in Chapter Three, I think it helps to consider ethics during the planning phase. Some of the principles that experienced benchmarkers recommend are the following:

- Do not ask others to tell you things you would not be willing to tell them.
- Do not misrepresent yourself or your company.
- Respect the proprietary rights of others.
- Review your company's ethics policy before starting benchmarking.
- Talk to your legal staff before visiting another company.

Concluding Thoughts

Now you have a basic plan. You know what you want to benchmark, how you will measure your practices against your partners, which organizations you will partner with, and how the data will be gathered. You are ready to implement the plan. But before moving to the next phase—which we discuss in the next chapter—you may want to go back through your plan one more time to be certain it will achieve what you want.

Chapter Three

Phase Two

Conducting the Study

Just as all leaders serve as the bridge between those
below them and those above them, the
organizational leaders at the highest level are the
bridge between those inside the organization and
the outside world.

—*Colonel Larry Donnithorne*,
The West Point Way of Leadership

People who are new to benchmarking are always surprised and
humbled by the willingness of partners to share. Successful organizations, especially those involved in the quality movement, are
eager to share their success stories because they are proud of what
they do. Companies like Motorola, Milliken, General Electric
(GE), and Xerox recognize that learning from the best is an essential element of the new economy. At GE, CEO Jack Welch ordered
the spread of best practices throughout the company, musing that
"best practices has legitimized plagiarism." But perhaps the most
cogent comment in this regard comes from the late Eric Hoffer,
who said: "In time of drastic change it is the learners who inherit
the future. The learned find themselves equipped to live in a world
that no longer exists." Indeed, those organizations that do not join
with their peers in the mutual sharing of performance data will find
that they are equipped for a world that no longer exists.

Purpose of Phase Two

Beginners to benchmarking often believe that the actual data gathering is the easiest part of the process. They think that a few phone calls or a trip to a partner's plant is all that is required and that it should not be all that difficult. Well, they are right! It *isn't* all that difficult. But the issue is not one of difficulty. Rather, the issue is one of a structured, understandable process and discipline on the part of those gathering the data. Specifically, to be successful in a benchmarking study a manager must understand the subject well enough to know if it will be better conducted as an internal project or an external effort and to establish a clear purpose for the study. Without these guidelines, the people conducting the study will not be clear about what is required, how much time is needed, or how difficult it will be to gather the data. Too often a benchmarking study fails not because of lack of commitment or energy but rather because of poor planning and unpreparedness.

A trap that lies in wait for any benchmarker, and especially the beginner, is impatience. Action always has more appeal than planning. People want to do something to correct a problem quickly. This is one of the reasons that what passes for benchmarking often is nothing more than "industrial tourism," that is, a group walk through someone else's plant or office, with questions asked as they come to mind, and everyone pleased and grateful for what they see. Of course, such an event can be interesting, even entertaining, but it is not benchmarking. The purpose of a benchmarking study is to get the answers to specific questions about your partners' operations in such a way that what you learn can be compared efficiently and meaningfully to your own operations.

Objectives of Phase Two

During Phase Two you will implement your benchmarking study plan. You will make certain that your assessment of your partners and of yourself will provide the knowledge you need for development and implementation of an improvement plan for your own operations. Phase Two is intended to ensure that you have a straightforward, dynamic study that will lead to meaningful comparison between you and your partners.

To achieve this objective, the benchmarking manager must be certain to do the following in a conscientious manner: validate the questions, make the final determination of who will collect the data, validate the data collection plan with a management champion, adhere to the ethics of benchmarking, and conduct the research. The rest of the chapter details these steps.

Validating the Questions

The first readiness test for a benchmarking study plan is to validate the questions you want to have answered. By "validating" I mean reviewing the questions you plan to ask to see if they will provide the information you need; that is, ensuring that the questionnaire—which you developed during Phase Two—covers the areas of interest. For example, are you interested in your partners' just-in-time system? Are inventory turns an important measure? Are your partners' customer involvement activities important? Ask yourself if your questions cover what you want to know about each of these areas. Will they help reveal your partners' best practices, both current and planned? And finally, will they reveal the performance measures that indicate the quantitative results that flow from the use of these best practices?

While reviewing your questionnaire you will also want to make sure that the questions don't rely on in-house jargon or professional jargon. Although professional shorthand may be familiar to people in your field, such jargon is almost always subject to the respondent's interpretation. A questionnaire should avoid confusion and be easy to execute. This is the best way to avoid problems midstream. For example, if your partners have to recheck data because the answer they gave was in response to something other than what you intended, your study process will suffer. A little extra effort before you start asking questions will provide confidence in your own and your partners' responses and allow you all to make meaningful comparisons of each other.

By validating your questions you will also be able to assess any difficulties your partners might encounter in attempting to provide the information you are requesting. In this way, you will avoid the most common complaint of experienced benchmarking organizations about beginners: they don't think about the difficulties of answering some of the questions they ask. The best way to do this is to answer your own questions. You may discover that it is not as easy to obtain some of the data as you had thought. If you can't answer your own questions, you can't expect anyone else to. If possible, have the people in your organization who are closest to the work answer the questions. This allows them to make suggestions on how to improve it. For example, if they had difficulty answering your questions and had to search out backup data that were not readily available, you can share with your partners how your people did it. This will help prevent your partners from turning down participation in your study because they cannot see a way to acquire some of the data. Giving them the method may just be what it takes to convince them to participate.

Another good reason for validating your questionnaire is that without the internal analysis and understanding that comes from answering your own questions, the chances are pretty good that your inquiry will lack the focus, purpose, and depth that your partners will expect. When your internal information is not known or at best has been ineffectively collected and organized, you are likely to appear disorganized and create the impression that you have not devoted the kind of time to the study that you expect from your partners. When you know your process well enough to be able to talk with great facility about it, your partners will feel confident that they are dealing with a well-prepared, knowledgeable group.

Remember also that requests that your partners increase the initially agreed-upon effort or time required are not likely to be received graciously. Even if your partners comply with such requests, they will not be likely to participate in subsequent bench-marking activities with you.

Validating your questionnaire in advance will go a long way toward avoiding these kinds of problems. By better understanding the scope of your investigation and the scope of the investment required, you will be more courteous and professional to your part-ners and the result will be more reliable and accurate data.

Determining Who Will Collect the Data

Before determining who will conduct the research, consider all the possibilities. Are you the right person to do it? Or is someone else in the organization better qualified to lead the effort? If so, would that person agree to do it? In fact, anyone who can contribute to the study or who will be responsible for the implementation of improvement actions should be given serious consideration. Some organizations have established benchmarking specialists who con-duct studies for internal customers and provide managers with con-sulting advice and training on how to start benchmarking projects. Unfortunately, few organizations are able to maintain this kind of resource and so most managers must learn the benchmarking process on their own. Actually, many benchmarking experts think that this situation is for the best. They believe that if benchmark-ing is to become a significant tool for an organization, it must be mastered and exploited by all the organization's managers. These experts argue that nothing can endure unless it becomes part of an organization's management system and that success at bench-marking is contingent upon a manager taking ownership of the process.

Unfortunately, however, most benchmarking projects require more skills and time than managers usually have available. This is the reason most often cited by benchmarking proponents for the use of outside consultants or teams. Yet, while advocating the value of teams, these same proponents caution managers that if they feel they are too busy to form their own benchmarking teams then they probably shouldn't be considering benchmarking at all!

The bottom line is that a manager starting a first benchmarking project will most likely wind up managing it personally. A manager launching a benchmarking project for the first time should always question if the right people are involved. If the answer is no, then the right people have to be found regardless of where they may be located.

Teams

Because most benchmarking studies require more than one person to complete the myriad tasks necessary, serious consideration should be given to establishing a team. A team provides the benefit of multiple points of view and experience. It also facilitates organizational learning both by internalizing the information acquired and by demonstrating through its members' efforts the importance of benchmarking to the rest of the organization. Because most work processes are not completed by one individual, it makes sense for all the people involved in a work process—or at least one representative of each group—to participate in determining how to change it. At Xerox, benchmarking teams are made up of a cross section of people and functions within the company. A typical Xerox benchmarking team consists of someone who understands the work process, someone who has analytical skills, another who has information-gathering talent, and, perhaps, someone who has team organization and facilitation competence. Camp (American Society for Training and Development, 1992) stresses that he prefers to have the manager who wants to improve a process within his or her division commission the team and determine the guidelines by which it will operate.

Establishing a team is not easy to do. Ed Lawler, director of the Center for Effective Organizations at the University of Southern California, puts it well: "Teams are like Ferraris" because "they're high performance," he says, but maintaining a high-performance machine requires high investment (Dumaine, 1994, p. 76).

The most effective teams include the people who will be responsible for implementing the processes that are developed as a result of the benchmarking study. This is because when the people who participate in a study are the same people who will implement the results, there is as much ownership in the results as there is in the effort to perform the study. Sally Sparhawk suggests the same thing. She recommends including those people who, later on, you may have to convince to implement the changes indicated. "We had a senior manager who wasn't real enthusiastic about some of the things we were doing. So we took him to a company with us. Things he thought were impossible, he saw the company doing. It turned him around" (American Society for Training and Development, 1992, p. 3). This kind of ownership also leads to a natural monitoring of the process because those who see the process as part of their work want to ensure that it continues to achieve or exceed the commitments they made to management (Watson, 1992–1993, p. 13).

The two most common kinds of teams are *task teams* and *work process teams*.

Task Teams. As its name suggests, the purpose of a task team is to accomplish a specific task. Therefore, a good place to start in selecting a team is to ask who is best qualified to study the subject at hand. Although benchmarking is time-consuming, it is essential to remember that it has the potential to be the most effective strategic tool you have ever used. There are three key roles on each task team: study project leader, functional and process experts, and staff support.

Study Project Leader. The study project leader might be you or a manager subordinate to you. Whatever your decision, the project leader is the principal liaison between the team and senior management. If a manager other than yourself is the customer for the benchmarking project, the project leader is the main contact between that customer and the team. He or she is also responsible for obtaining benchmarking training for the team, leading the team and coordinating the planning, scheduling the activities and directing efforts, controlling the budget for the project, leading meetings, and monitoring the team's progress.

Functional and Process Experts. As already noted, teams are especially effective if their members come from the pool of functional and process experts close to the study subject because the team's purpose is to identify process improvements that will produce better results than the organization's current work process. Obviously, the operators of the work process are best equipped to bring this understanding to the team. Therefore, it is best to have some of these people on the team help develop the instruments for data collection, make contact with the benchmarking partners, schedule the data collection trips, and especially evaluate the data, identify the performance gaps, and develop the action plans. These functional and process experts are also the people who should present the team's findings to senior management. In his book *Business Process Benchmarking*, Camp (1995, p. 179) says that in addition to understanding the benchmarking process, "team members should possess analytical, research, process documentation, and team facilitation skills." By analytical skills he means engineering or technical skills; by research skills he means interest in conducting information research. This latter skill can be provided outside the team in the form of specialized staff support. Finally, team facilitation skills are often overlooked, particularly by organizations that have not had the advantage of total quality management, but these skills are especially important to a benchmarking team's success during the study's start-up phase and during data evaluation.

Staff Support. From time to time during the study you will have to tap into your organization's staff support resources to assist in data processing, training, acquisition of financial information, legal counsel, and production of the report documents. Because these kind of resources are needed "when they are needed," you or the project leader will have to clear the way by making sure the team knows about these experts and that the experts themselves are willing and able to respond. For example, benchmarking training will have to be provided to the team (and perhaps to your partners), conflicts with "need to know" restrictions and other security policies will have to be resolved in advance with finance and information management, and the legal and ethical limitations of benchmarking will have to be clearly understood by everyone on the team. If your legal staff is not familiar with benchmarking then they had better get up to speed quickly. Kent Johnson, corporate counsel with Texas Instruments (TI), says, "When I first came to TI, lawyers counseled senior management. We set the 'rules' and management enforced them. We had the 'you can't trust the salesmen' attitude." But now Texas Instruments must provide legal advice to every employee engaged in benchmarking. "Lawyers need to become knowledgeable about benchmarking," Johnson says, "because everybody is doing it"—even lawyers (Scheffler and Powers, 1992–1993, pp. 27–30).

At Lyondell Petrochemical Company the legal department began process benchmarking in 1992 with a focus on analyzing key process from the perspective of client satisfaction and determining where innovation is possible through the elimination or modification of tasks or processes, avoiding closed-loop thinking that concentrates only on improving existing procedures, and addressing organizational concerns that are not focused in any one client group.

We will talk later in this chapter about conducting library research, but it is important to point out here the significance of the organization's library. The library is a staff resource from the point of view of research expertise and counsel and is also an entryway to the more than five thousand electronic databases available in the United States. These databases can provide extensive benchmarking data. If your organization does not have a library or if the library staff hasn't the time to support your benchmarking team, remember that public libraries and service bureaus provide the same resources. Seeking out these services and making them accessible to the team is the project leader's responsibility.

Work Process Teams. As has been stressed, the people best equipped to conduct a benchmarking study are those who perform the actual work of the process being benchmarked. There are two reasons for their value. First, they understand the process better than anyone else and for that reason can best evaluate the benchmarking partners' practices. Second, if the study leads to a change in the work process, these people will have to make that change. Their very participation in the study and data gathering will help eliminate any resistance later on. The participative approach creates a new scenario. Rather than "This is how *you* are going to do it," the feeling becomes "This is how *we* are going to do it" (Watson, 1992–1993, p. 13).

Furthermore, the expression "No one is as smart as all of us," is the basis for the value of a team evaluating its own work and that of its competitors. These people are more likely to see the benchmarking process as part of their work. They will thus use the data they gather to assure that their work process continues to meet or exceed their management's expectations. For example, at AT&T Bell Laboratories when an area has been targeted for benchmarking, a team is established to conduct the data collection and analysis. The team includes members from the R&D benchmarking support function and members solicited from process teams across Bell Labs whose functions are aligned with the benchmarking area (Bean and Gros, 1992).

The creation of a work process team to benchmark doesn't mean total delegation. Too often management launches a team into a benchmarking project in a vacuum, offering it little or no training or support and later wondering why results were not achieved. Getting a work process team started on a benchmarking process is the easy part; the difficult part is staying with the team and removing the barriers to its progress.

Training

Smart people can get pretty good at benchmarking on their own; nevertheless, it is risky to attempt benchmarking without some formal training. For one thing, training gives you credibility with your partners. Since time is critical to everyone these days, you don't want yourself or your team to be perceived as casual or, worse, unprepared. As Camp points out, "Benchmarking partners will absolutely want to know how well prepared you are and how you plan to conduct the study" (Kinni, 1994, p. 32). On the flip side of that argument, Dennis Percher says, "I believe everyone should have an awareness of benchmarking but not everyone should take the training" because it would be a waste of time. He explains, "I've had people come back a year after they've taken the training to take it again now that they are going to do a benchmarking project" (American Society for Training and Development, 1992, p. 2). At AT&T, management believes the best time for training is when a work group is doing benchmarking. Percher points out, "It is important that people understand benchmarking is not just looking around. When you make the visits and talk to people, and ask them the questions, you have to make sure you've got the right company, and know your own processes well enough so that any nuance or difference in another organization's process becomes evident" (American Society for Training and Development, 1992, p. 2). Training is important because as Bogan and English (1994, p. 73) point out, benchmarking "is not conceptually difficult but it is extremely detail-rich."

Training is available from a variety of sources. Many university extension programs offer training programs, usually modeled after the Xerox and AT&T two-day courses. Successful quality and benchmarking organizations like Milliken, Federal Express, DEC, and Xerox offer their own programs for sale and even provide start-up consulting. Of course, a growing number of consulting firms and individual consultants offer hands-on services including training. In addition, the American Productivity and Quality Center, based in Houston, Texas, offers workshops throughout the country.

Whatever the source of your training, whether externally or internally developed, the curriculum must cover the following issues:

- A review of benchmarking and the process model to follow
- The uses and applications of benchmarking, including terms and tools
- The roles and responsibilities of team members
- Project management tools and techniques
- Selection of subjects and partners
- Data-collection methods and procedures
- Methods of conducting site visits
- Legal issues and the ethics of benchmarking
- Implementation of action plans and management follow-up

Consultants

In many situations consultants can be very useful to a benchmarking effort. Some of the country's leading organizations have successfully used consultants to design their surveys and gather the data, particularly when their benchmarking partners were hesitant about providing detailed information. A consulting firm can usually defuse these kinds of situations by promising confidentiality. For example, consultants have traditionally been used for compensation surveys, which have been conducted for years—since long before anyone used the term *benchmarking*.

An increasing number of consulting firms have entered the benchmarking field and many of them are quite good. In addition, with all the downsizing, "there are a lot of individuals with excellent skills around, people who could really help a small company" with benchmarking, as Bob Camp points out (Kinni, 1994, p. 32). Although it may take some time to find these people, the effort would certainly be offset by the cost savings of not using one of the larger consulting firms.

Thus, although the decision to use a consultant can be a very good one, I do not think it wise to limit your study exclusively to a consultant because you need the benefit of some firsthand information. Also, although consultants can be very effective, if someone else does the work for you, you will be so engaged at both the beginning and the end of the project that there will be no "value-added" to the process. Often these benchmarking experts take up so much of your time at both these moments that you gain little from their help. At the beginning they need your time to learn about your operation and they will only know what you tell them. Unless these experts have remarkable insight they will not have the experience necessary to know what questions to ask next, as would an experienced professional. At the end of the study, you will have to provide additional input in order to understand the results of the study and how best to put them to use. And even after all of that, when you ask deeper, more probing questions, it is likely that they won't have all the answers. Of course, the exception is when the benchmarking experts are also functional experts in the subject area being studied. For example, Nolan, Norton, and Company in Boston, Compass America Inc. in Reston, Virginia, and Real Decisions Corporation in Darien, Connecticut, are the primary providers of client-server benchmarking services to the information technology industry (Caldwell, 1995, p. 82). Between them they serve over three hundred clients and provide accurate feedback on how each client-server system stacks up against both competitors and companies in comparable industries.

I advise as much caution in choosing a consultant as you would use in choosing any vendor. Check references and experience. Do not hesitate to follow up on those references. And even when a consultant is used, be certain that you know the names of all the partner organizations participating in your study and look for assurances from these partners that they know you are a participant. Finally, carefully consider all the security implications involved for your organization in exchanging proprietary information through a third party.

As noted in Chapter One, Pfizer reported miscommunication and misinterpretation of data as major concerns in the benchmarking process. For example, Pfizer found that different companies meant different things when they talked about "alignment with the business." In one company, alignment meant alignment with a division's business goals; at another it meant alignment of goals and strategies at the corporate level. Pfizer also found that surveys undertaken by third parties did not help to overcome the miscommunication and that it was best to talk directly to one's benchmarking partners.

Validating the Plan with a Management Champion

The final step before launching your plan is to review it with a management champion. A champion is someone who possesses credibility and has access to senior staff. This person can be an advocate and supporter for your study and its potential recommendations and action plans as well as act as a sounding board for management's apprehensions and expectations. Such a person might be a member of the senior staff (that is optimal). That person might be you. One reason for a management champion is that it is very likely that some managers in your organization will be resistent to a benchmarking study, especially if they think its results might be threatening to them. Early buy-in by the management most affected by the results will allow you to counter that kind of resistance. This will make communications and implementation of the study's results easier and will assure management support at the beginning so that you will be able to obtain the resources and time you need.

Weyerhaeuser Corporation, Seattle, has identified eight specific responsibilities for managers who are supporting a benchmarking study (Karch, 1992–1993). They form a good guide for a management champion's behavior:

1. Emphasize the need for setting the expectations.
2. Select members of the team and a leader (if he or she does not directly lead the activity).
3. Provide the necessary resources, time, and support to the team members to allow them to do a quality job.
4. Set the guidelines within which the benchmarking effort is to take place.
5. Ensure that adequate training is provided to the benchmarking team members.
6. Make necessary contacts with other companies (because of the weight that the leadership position carries).
7. Receive the results and recommendations with an open mind and make every effort to implement the most important of them.
8. Recognize and reward team members for their contributions.

Adhering to the Ethics of Benchmarking

The success of a benchmarking study is entirely dependent on the strictest professional conduct by the partners. Effective benchmarking requires the careful building of an environment between organizations of trust, cooperation, and learning, and developing such mutual respect requires more than a common process. Therefore, never misrepresent yourself or your company. Never ask others to tell you things you would not tell about your own organization. Always respect your partners' proprietary rights. In general, adhere to benchmarking's golden rule: "Don't do unto competition in data gathering what you wouldn't want to have them do unto you." In some cases the legal and moral lines may not be clear, but the following list provides a pretty good place to start drawing lines in the sand:

- Do not make false representation about yourself, your employment, or the purpose of your research.
- Do not obtain competitive products illegally.
- Do not provide proprietary data to other organizations without following your own company's policy.
- Do not entice suppliers to divulge information by promising business.
- Do not discuss pricing (unless your company specifically allows you to do so).
- Do not ask for or obtain data on proprietary products or processes.

One-Way Benchmarking

Gathering intelligence about a competitor without having to share is both a rare occurrence and a challenge. It is rare because it is such an easy way to obtain data and requires a high degree of trust by the competitor. Most often such a one-way flow of data is achieved only by hiring a professional database searcher or third-party consultant. Intelligence gathering is challenging because the maintaining of contacts within a competitor who willingly provide one-way information, unique and precious as it is, may be looked upon with suspicion and skepticism by people in both organizations. Using such contacts is ethical and legal as long as you have not misrepresented yourself. You will also want to guard against inadvertently sharing data about yourself without reciprocity; this has been known to happen. For example, suppose a competitor requests not data about your performance but "just the metrics you use." This may seem a small request, but your metrics may easily provide insights into your operations that are not part of the public record. Inadvertent revelations aside, the only other important caveat about one-way benchmarking is not to use it as a means of pressuring a partner to reveal that organization's proprietary data.

Maintaining a Standard of Behavior

Even putting aside the moral issue, there is a practical reason for maintaining a behavioral standard that is above reproach. Simply put, the consequences of illegally or unethically gathered data can be severe for your organization and possibly for you as an employee. Kent Johnson, TI's counsel, advises setting some rules and then following them "without exception" and "insisting that your benchmarking partners do so as well." He recalls Supreme Court Justice Oliver Wendell Holmes, who said that when businesspeople get together, "they are probably up to no good and are talking about evil things" (Day, 1993, p. 52). That is the catch: the very essence of benchmarking is businesspeople talking with one another and when the more zealous among us start speaking of "stealing shamelessly," equally zealous lawyers raise their eyebrows. Johnson cautions that benchmarking partners firmly assure each other that there will be no agreements in restraint of trade or collusion or violations of intellectual property rights.

It is important that benchmarking organizations resolve these problems for themselves because the alternative will be governmental regulators imposing their set of rules on us. For example, although as benchmarking partners Ford and General Motors could learn much from one another, any plan to exchange information would have to be carefully considered because the two are in such strong competition. D. Andrew Byrne, attorney with Pennington, Wilkinson, and Dunlap, P.A., Florida, notes that there are some antitrust risks from the Justice Department. But he quickly adds that there is a bigger risk in not benchmarking. "Benchmarking is such a powerful tool, you cannot afford not to do it" (Scheffler and Powers, 1992–1993).

Four Guidelines

Based on their own consulting and studies of benchmarking organizations, Spendolini and Thompson (1992, p. 13) recommend four ethical guidelines:

1. Do not press for information that is reported as or appears to be sensitive or proprietary.

2. Conduct the benchmarking investigation through the regular hierarchy of the target organization. Work downward through the organizational strata until contact is made with the source people for the desired information.

3. Always inform your prospective benchmark partners of your true intentions and purposes for benchmarking. Don't mask your intentions. Ensure that any third parties (such as students or consultants) who are benchmarking under your aegis represent themselves clearly as your agents or representatives.

4. Never divulge the information you collect from your benchmarking sources to any other party unless explicit written permission to do so has been secured.

Unacceptable Practices

The four guidelines are applicable in almost any kind of partner-to-partner exchange. But there are certain unacceptable data-gathering practices that require more detailed comment.

- *Job interviews.* Candidates like to impress potential employers but it is unacceptable for you to take advantage of the situation by enticing the candidate to divulge proprietary information during a job interview. It is best to tell applicants immediately that you are not interested in any information considered confidential by their current employers.

- *Hires from competitors.* Employees of competitors may be recruited for their abilities, skills, and talent but not for their competitive information.

- *Trade shows and conferences.* Although you do not need to reveal your identity to competitors at their booths if the information they are sharing is being furnished to all attenders, it is inappropriate to misrepresent yourself for the purpose of gathering information.

- *Phony bids.* It is unethical to ask a loyal customer to put out a proposal request to your competitors to solicit bids on parts, technology, pricing, and so on for the sole purpose of obtaining data for you.

- *Suppliers.* Although it is acceptable to check the output of a key competitor by asking his supplier about the volume he ships, it is unacceptable to entice a supplier to divulge information by suggesting that you will use him only if he shares the information with you.

- *Internal telephone directories and organization charts.* It is unacceptable to obtain through misrepresentation the internal telephone directories or organization charts of an organization without prior authorization.

- *Aerial photographs.* In most communities in the United States it is illegal to take aerial photographs of a competitor's facilities; it is a form of invasion of privacy.

- *Plant tours.* If a plant does not provide tours to the public, ethics require that you reveal your own affiliation to the host organization before you take a tour there. Thus it would be inappropriate to accompany a noncompetitor partner on that company's tour of your competitor's operations without identifying yourself.

- *Reverse engineering.* Reverse engineering is an acceptable benchmarking tool as long as the product is obtained legally. Similarly, reverse process evaluation is an equally good tool to use.

To the new benchmarker, the legal and ethical requirements may at first seem overwhelming and limiting but as Gerald O'Brien, associate general counsel for Lyondell Petrochemical Company, says, "Benchmarking is like rock and roll; it's here to stay" (Scheffler and Powers, 1992–1993, p. 30).

The Benchmarking Code of Conduct

Perhaps the best guide to follow is the Benchmarking Code of Conduct, a set of principles that has been adopted by the companies that belong to the International Benchmarking Clearinghouse of the American Productivity and Quality Center. The code consists of seven principles:

1. *The principle of legality*. Avoid discussions or actions that might lead to or imply an interest in restraint of trade, market or customer allocation schemes, price fixing, dealing arrangements, bid rigging, bribery, or misappropriation. Do not discuss costs with competitors if costs are an element of pricing.

2. *The principle of exchange*. Be willing to provide the same level of information that you request from another in a benchmarking exchange.

3. *The principle of confidentiality*. Treat a benchmarking interchange as something confidential to the individuals and organizations involved. Information obtained must not be communicated outside the partnering organizations without prior consent of the participants. An organization's participation in a study should not be communicated externally without its permission.

4. *The principle of use*. Use information obtained through benchmarking only for the purpose of improving operations within the partnering companies themselves. External use or communication of a benchmarking partner's name with their data or observed practices requires permission of that partner. Do not, as a consultant or a client, extend one company's benchmarking study findings to another without the first company's permission.

5. *The principle of first-party contact*. Initiate contacts whenever possible through a benchmarking contact designated by the partner company and obtain mutual agreement with the contact on any exchange of communications or change in responsibility to other parties.

6. *The principle of third-party contact*. Obtain an individual's permission before providing that person's name in response to a contact request.

7.   *The principle of preparation.* Demonstrate commitment to the efficiency and effectiveness of the benchmarking process with adequate preparation at each process step, particularly during initial partner contact.

Conducting the Research

Although many sources of information are available they can all be boiled down into two types: internal and external. As we explained in Chapter Two, internal research is the easiest to perform. Your own functional experts are accessible, sharing data between internal generic operations is common, and organization's libraries and databases are available with relative ease.

External information is more difficult to access. This information comes from the public domain or is derived through original research.

Information in the Public Domain

Much of the information you want (indeed, perhaps all of it) is available to you in the public domain. From stockbroker analyses to government reports to annual reports and articles in periodicals, a broad array of sources is capable of yielding vast amounts of statistical and anecdotal information. Even if it does not provide all the answers you seek, this kind of research is essential before you make the final determination of which organizations would make the best partners and what questions you should be asking them. And it might yield all the information you require. As an example of the value of a literature search, compare the public comments (from distinctly different sources) about the administrative overhead of two insurance firms. The first is from Torchmark Corporation's 1990 annual report: "Improvements have been made [by Liberty National Life Insurance Company, a Torchmark subsidiary] in the processing time for issuing policies and for paying claims. Instead of incoming telephone calls going to various departments of the company, calls are being directed to a centralized unit where response time and quality of response can be controlled. In order to minimize error and improve efficiency, changes have been made in the premium collection procedures of the company. In addition to, and partly as a result of improved service, administrative expenses declined $2 million to $47 million, or 11.7 percent of premium income in 1990, compared to 12.8 percent of premium income in 1989" (p. 6). Compare that to the comments of American General: "[American General's home-service life insurance unit's] expenses are nearly double those of Torchmark's home-service unit" (McConagle, 1992, p. 34).

Original Research

Although original research always begins in the public domain it extends beyond it to a direct reaching out to benchmarking partners. By starting with published material from corporations or other applicable agents, such as professional societies, industry watchers, and technical associations, you can capture relevant information that will produce leads to additional information sources. For example, a review of an article about a potential competitor in a national newspaper may lead you to that firm's annual report, which may in turn lead you to the technical papers presented by that organization's engineering staff at public conferences. From there you may learn about the published articles of their vendors or their contributions to the competitor's product performance. And from there you may look into what the analysts are writing about that organization. If you have not by then learned enough to be able to compare your comparable practices, you will want to explore further how your two operations are similar or dissimilar and why. This exploration can only be accomplished by reaching out to the organization in an open exchange of information. There are basically three ways to do this: mail survey, telephone survey, and site visit.

Although each of these original research methods stands alone, the likelihood is that you will use all three in a sort of step-by-step or building-block approach as you exchange data and build mutual confidence and trust.

Mail Surveys. The mail survey is perhaps the most commonly used method for gathering large samples of data because it provides an easy means for partners to respond to specific questions and, of course, is reasonably inexpensive. Many benchmarking organizations begin their data gathering with surveys, using these data to help them screen partners for follow-up questioning and visits.

Mail surveys are usually limited to a targeted set of partners but there is real value to considering a broader target population, especially when you intend to limit your research to a mail survey alone. In this case, keep in mind that you can usually obtain appropriate mailing lists from your trade association membership roster, trade publication lists, and the mailing lists of your vendors. Once you have settled on a target population to which to send your mail survey, the challenge is to achieve a reasonable rate of return on your investment.

Hotels and airlines often offer drawings for free trips and hotel stays as incentives for completing surveys because it provides them with data about their competitors from their customers. Although a prize is sometimes an appropriate incentive, the most practical and usually most successful means of encouraging recipients to respond to a benchmarking survey is to offer them a copy of the results.

When you use a mail survey you should consider the following ways of improving response rates:

- *For small populations, telephone in advance.* The most practical reason for calling before mailing a survey is to identify the right person to send it to. Furthermore, in addition to giving your potential partners the opportunity to ask you questions about the survey you will be able to screen out those who clearly will not respond, saving yourself the cost of the survey and postage. Also, there will come a point when you will want to ask some of these potential partners follow-up questions or arrange a site visit; these are easier to arrange if you have already established contact.
- *Personalize your request and sign the cover letter.* If you and your partners have not met or spoken on the telephone, a personal

letter is the next best thing. The letter can explain why your partner was selected, suggesting that your mailing is not some mass exercise where a single response will not be missed. Also, by sharing your name, title, and contact information, you give the survey a human face and let your partners know that you are open to be contacted by those who wish to make the effort.

• *Send the materials by first-class mail.* Mailing first class does three things. First, it makes it less likely that your survey will be lost in the piles of junk mail that individuals and organizations receive daily. Second, it tells your potential partners that the contents are important to you. Third, it tells them that their attention, and in turn their response, is also important to you.

• *Make your questionnaire attractive and easy to complete.* How many surveys have you received in the mail and discarded simply because you didn't understand what to do with them? How many others did you try to complete but then abandon because they were too long or too complex? If you want those who receive your survey to provide you with information about themselves and their operations, it will go a long way if the survey itself is attractive. For example, it is a good idea to print on colored paper so that it stands out from other mail. Also, a document that is on one sheet of paper, folded over, is preferable to a stapled multipage document.

Your survey should also be easy to follow. That is, questions should flow logically and the instructions should be clear (examples always help). Finally, it is best to avoid open-ended questions. A survey completed alone is more enticing when the format limits response options.

Include a self-addressed stamped envelope (SASE). Obviously, an SASE makes it more convenient and therefore easier for respondents to return the completed questionnaire. But it also says two other important things to a potential partner. First, it tells them that you know their time is important and are trying to minimize the investment they will need to make to participate. Second, and perhaps most significant, it says that their response is so important to you that you are making the task as easy as you can for them.

Telephone Surveys. A telephone interview is an extremely significant tool to a benchmarking organization both as a means of following up on information acquired from research and mail surveys, and as a simple, convenient, and inexpensive means of conducting an original study. However, a telephone interview cannot be conducted spontaneously. Like any other method of data gathering, it requires a plan. An updated version of the mail survey or your original questionnaire are the two most likely structures. Having a set of predetermined questions at hand will help assure that your partners' time is not wasted and that you will acquire the information you need.

One use of a telephone survey is to follow up on a mail survey. Your mail survey was likely limited to multiple choice or scaled response options, and a telephone interview is an excellent method for clarifying the responses. The kinds of questions you ask on the telephone will be more open-ended, encouraging your partner to talk and share the thinking behind the survey responses.

The second use of a telephone survey is as original research. Instead of starting with a mail survey, your first contact with potential partners will be by telephone and if the study does not require a face-to-face dialogue, it may be the only contact you have with your partners. The sources for identifying potential telephone survey targets are the same as for a mail survey, although you will require a larger sample because the number of organizations who are willing to participate will be lower. Therefore, in looking for personal contacts, seek leads from any former employees of potential partners, from your salespeople, and from any benchmarking network sources you may have, both internal and external. In addition to the network contacts you may have outside your organization, check out your trade association directory and the names of authors of recent articles on the subjects you want to benchmark.

Sometimes you can develop appropriate leads by contacting the telephone operator of your potential partner and asking who could best answer your questions.

Here are some good guidelines to follow when conducting a telephone interview:

1. Review in advance all the data you have researched about the organization.

2. Get a contact name and schedule the interview with that person in advance.

3. Be prepared to tell your contact who referred you, using either a specific name, an article, or an association.

4. Begin the conversation by introducing yourself and explaining who you are and why you are calling.

5. Play a little to your contact's ego—we all like to talk about ourselves and our organization's successes.

6. Follow your questionnaire, but remember open-ended questions will allow your contact to talk.

7. Don't be too quick to respond to an answer or to ask the next question. Too often we miss the second level of detail because we don't let the person talk. Learn to wait, to pause between responses, as though you expect more.

8. Provide an incentive to your contact (again, the results of your study is best).

9. If your objective is to visit your partner, take the opportunity to request a visit and confirm the agenda.

Site Visits. There are many times when it is advantageous to visit your partner's site either to observe a work process or just to get to know your partner better. Personal visits with a partner's representatives to observe a work site or work process are the most powerful benchmarking experiences because meeting with the people who actually conduct work processes and influence the outcomes of the processes being benchmarked provide an opportunity to confirm research as well as to gather data and assess veracity and candor. A successful site visit is constructed with careful attention to three elements: preparation before the visit, behavior during the visit, and debriefing after the visit.

Before the Visit. Before you actually visit a site there are several things for you to consider to be sure that you are prepared. Determine the most appropriate person to contact at the partner's organization and stress to that person your interest in uncovering industry best practices. Make your contact a professional-to-professional dialogue to create an initial interest in sharing information and agree upon an itinerary for the visit. Identify the team to make the visit and agree upon everyone's role during the visit. If possible, conduct a mock interview so that all can become familiar with their roles. You will want to make sure your questions are not leading but instead solicit the information you don't already possess. Share your questions in advance and be prepared to answer why you are asking a particular question. Have a set of answers for your own organization ready to share with your partner. If proprietary data are to be exchanged, be certain that your partner has agreed to the exchange, and that you have your own organization's approval. Finally, prepare a portfolio of brochures about your organization to leave behind.

During the Visit. To get the most of your time during a visit, always begin with an exchange of business cards so that everyone knows who's who and who does what, and state the objective of the visit. Use your eyes and ears and document what you see and hear as thoroughly as possible, asking the appropriate questions, using "jargon" where it will help—but avoiding your organizational jargon and acronyms—and always probing for the root causes of what you have learned.

After the Visit. When the visit is over, you will want to be certain that you properly debrief the team and that you document your visit for both the team and management.

The objective is to ensure that your benchmarking effort is successful by effectively covering all the before, during, and after issues. If you do this effectively you will be able to build a relationship with your partner that you can both replicate in the future. These eight guidelines may be helpful:

1.   *Select a team for the visit.* Identify the person at your partner organization who will be responsible for your visit and negotiate with this contact the itinerary, including the number of people from your organization who will make the visit. There is no perfect number for a site visit team, but you never want to show up with more persons than your partner expects. I personally recommend a minimum of three people and a maximum of five. (Costs aside, a larger group may appear to be "ganging up" on your partner. In addition, you may not be able to use everyone productively.) The minimum number of three is to fulfill three important roles:

The interviewer is the person who will actually ask the questions. The objective is to keep the inquiry as conversational as possible. Experience has shown that a dialogue process is the most effective means of obtaining information. To establish a rapport of dialogue the interviewer should be free to look at the persons responding to questions.

The recorder's job is solely to record the responses. Because you want the interviewer to be free to maintain a conversational tone, it is valuable to have another individual do this job. This process will go more smoothly if you follow your questionnaire.

The observer does not participate in the conversation but merely observes the partner's representatives, paying particular attention to nonverbal behavior. For example, did the interviewer move too quickly to the next question and therefore miss an opportunity for more information? The observer may note that this particular question represents an opportunity for follow up. Did any response seem insincere or limited—might there have been an attempt to hold back something? An observer can be particularly valuable if your partner is from a different cultural environment than your own. For example, the Japanese possess a more reserved method of conversing.

2. *Make sure you have sufficient time.* When making reservations for the visit, be sure that your travel schedule guarantees that you will arrive on time. (If you are not familiar with the directions to your partner's location, build in some "getting lost" time.) Next, be certain that the schedule allows you to stay as long as needed to complete the visit. It is a good idea to allow sufficient time and flexibility so that in the event the visit has to be extended you have the time. If your partner is also a customer, and you didn't use your sales rep or account manager as the intermediary to help set up the visit, now is the time to contact him or her. At the very least a sales rep is entitled to know that you will be visiting his account. But for purposes of credibility and relationships, you also might want the sales rep to accompany you on the visit.

3. *Obtain prior approval for the questions you will ask.* It is important that you and your partner agree on the questions you intend to ask, including those relating to best practices. Prior approval helps keep you within a time frame by allowing your partner to preassemble the information you are requesting. You will make this easier if you use your "industry jargon" to facilitate the exchange but be certain that your organization's specific jargon or acronyms do not creep in. Also, although follow-up questions for the purpose of clarification are appropriate, it is inappropriate to add new subjects without your partner's permission.

4. *Arrange tours in advance.* If you wish to observe a work process or a manufacturing process, the tour should be prearranged with your partner. Usually plant tours or facility walk-throughs require the approval of operations management and the company's legal department. You always want to make such requests in advance out of common courtesy to your host. You never want to put your host in a position that may result in embarrassment or a

feeling of being compromised. Even if a last-minute request is not denied, it will certainly intrude on your relationship with your partner, which is still being formed and probably fragile.

5.   *Be sure you have a "game plan."* Bring with you an outline of the topics you want to cover to act as a guide for the visit and the exchange of information—as already suggested, it is best to follow your questionnaire—which should be consistent with your agreements with your partner. You should also have on hand your purpose statement and all relevant data about your partner. Also bring your own answers to the questions you are going to ask: remember, benchmarking is a reciprocal process and you want to demonstrate your openness by volunteering these data. As you plan this part of your visit be sure to consider the possible need for follow-up conversations should you wish to add questions to those originally negotiated. In other words, anticipate what you might learn and how the conversation might go well enough that you are prepared to take advantage of the situation.

6.   *Know how you will retain observations if note taking is not convenient.* During your visit you will need to take notes and ask clarifying questions. However, taking notes may not be an easy thing to do during a plant tour. If this is the case you will have to use your eyes and ears carefully and remember key points; then document them as soon after the tour as possible. It helps sometimes to say out loud—especially to a member of your team—those things you find significant. Immediately after the tour, attempt to obtain clarification of your observations while everything is still fresh in your mind. Of course, be prepared to discuss your equivalent data and information, and to offer a reciprocal visit and tour if appropriate. In fact, it is best to set up reciprocal visits right then and there. As quickly as possible after the visit is over, debrief the team members. You will want to get to a private place away from your partner's facility to discuss everyone's observations and ideas by reviewing the responses to each question as well as the notations of the observer. A hotel lobby, public library, even a local park can work quite well. If you're leaving town, the club room of a frequent flyer

lounge is often a good place for such a session. Regardless of the location, you will want to conduct the debriefing quickly, while everything is still fresh in everyone's mind.

7.   *Know your legal and ethical obligations*. Before a visit to your partner, especially if it will involve a plant tour or work process observation, it is important that you review your organization's ethics policy and talk to your legal department. You are certain to be asked to sign a nondisclosure agreement and you should understand what limits your organization requires of you. The point is never to violate the law and to stick to the highest ethical standards. Both you and your partner should agree to a code of ethical conduct. (For more on this, see the previous section on the ethics of benchmarking.)

8.   *Document your visit with a thank-you note and a report*. Once back at your office, you will want to thank your partner for his time and cooperation. It is best to do this both informally with a handshake and smile and formally with a written note. Send copies of it to the appropriate management in your partner's organization. It is likely that you will want to confirm the accuracy of your notes from the visit; include that request as part of your written thank-you. Of course, you also need to document the visit in a written trip report for your own project leader and your management champion.

Informal Visits.   Although formal process-to-process benchmarking is the main source of information for identifying best practices, sometimes an informal visit is better. These kinds of visits occur most often between senior managers for the purpose of exposing them to different practices to assist them in deciding if they wish to pursue formal benchmarking. They are sometimes called "feel good trips." Informal visits have some particular characteristics. For example, the participants are senior managers. There are no specific objectives to the meeting. There is no previsit questionnaire. There is usually only one attender, sometimes two. The meeting has results-oriented focus rather than a process-oriented one. Finally, there is little postvisit documentation or communication.

Panel Interviews. Another method of benchmarking exchange between partners is the panel interview. This is the method used in strategic benchmarking. Because strategic benchmarking focuses on broader, more strategic issues, it doesn't usually require a site visit. It relies instead on face-to-face meetings of all the partners to exchange data on a specific subject or two. Usually the location of the session rotates between partner sites, although many organizations that participate in panel discussions prefer to meet at neutral locations. Generally, panel interviews are conducted by a third party consultant and the partners share the costs. All of the guidelines presented earlier in this chapter on the use of consultants are applicable here. In addition, panel interview sessions should adhere to the following rules:

1. Participants should know the purpose and objectives of the discussion in advance as well as the meeting's agenda and the specific questions to be discussed.

2. It is best if the consultant functions as the facilitator or coordinator. If the consultant is not skilled in this way then all the participants need to agree on a person to perform that function.

3. The consultant is responsible for establishing and clarifying the procedure for documenting the discussion between partners, for exchanging the information that will be shared, and for maintaining the confidentiality of the exchange outside of the group.

Concluding Thoughts

Once the necessary data have been obtained and you have returned to your own office, the really difficult work of benchmarking begins. Like almost everything else in life, asking the questions turns out to be the easy part. Interpreting and validating the answers so that you can make effective judgments are the more difficult but ultimately more rewarding tasks.

Chapter Four

Phase Three

Analyzing the Data

The only things worth learning are the things you
learn after you know it all.
　　　　　—*Harry S Truman, quoted in* Plain Speaking,
　　　　　　　　　　　　　　　　Merle Miller

In his enthralling chronicle of baseball—which explains why the
game demands intellectual energy, logic, and hard work of the men
who participate in it—George Will (1990) begins Men at Work
with a profile of team manager Tony La Russa of the Oakland A's.
Appropriately, the first picture Will paints of La Russa is in a meeting with his first-level managers where they are preparing for the
first game in a series with the Boston Red Sox. Will describes in
broad detail their disciplined and detailed process of analyzing and
evaluating months of statistics that reveal Boston's strengths, weaknesses, tendencies, and preferences. The description of La Russa's
team meeting is a wonderful lesson for anyone aspiring to manage
a baseball team—or beginning the process of benchmarking data
analysis.

Purpose of Phase Three

Benchmarking data analysis begins with organizing the information you have gathered into a manageable format. Unless the data
are laid out in a clear fashion that makes them easy to examine and
the correlations simple to follow, you won't be able to make an
evaluation. So the first step is to organize your information in a
manner with which you are comfortable. Once that is done, start

your analysis by reviewing all the information for its applicability to your study, its thoroughness, and its accuracy. To do this, ask yourself three questions: Do you have all the information you planned to obtain? Do all the data apply to your study or do you have more information than you need? Is the information correct?

Do you have all the information you planned to obtain? It is not unusual to discover that some of the information you set out to get is missing. If this is the case, you will have to correct it! The most common reason for not being able to identify performance gaps—which is a goal of benchmarking, as will be discussed later—is some sort of problem with the data. Usually, a problem develops because the data are either incomplete or inaccurate. When this is the case you have no choice but to recontact your partners to revalidate, correct, or update their responses to your questions. This shouldn't be a problem because a benchmarking partner expects the other to follow up—most often on the telephone—to verify the accuracy of the information provided. Benchmarking partners do this because it is to their benefit to ensure that the data are as reliable as possible because they too will be using the results.

Do all the data apply to your study or do you have more information than you need? Beginning benchmarkers are often surprised to learn how much information their research has produced, especially if they have used the full spectrum of sources—library research, surveys, interviews, and site visits. In fact, it is not uncommon during a site visit for a benchmarking study to acquire a life of its own, expanding beyond its original scope and resulting in the capture of extensive, unexpected information. In a way, a benchmarking study can be likened to the process a fisherman employs when he casts his net broadly and drags it deeply. His target fish may be halibut but his net will probably also capture sea bass, sturgeon, tuna—perhaps even some species he knows he cannot keep, like porpoise. Sorting out the fish he wants from those he doesn't and separating those he can sell whole from those that require special processing are not easy tasks—and they take time.

So it is with benchmarking. You are likely to gather more data than you expected to. If you discover that the data you have gathered provide information that is actually more valuable than that needed to reach your original objective, it may be profitable to take a new tack for your study. The benchmarking model is iterative— you can always go back and revisit ground you have already covered and by so doing, cover new ground. However, it should also be noted that beginning benchmarkers are probably better off deciding to put aside the unexpected data until a later time and proceeding first with their original plan.

Is the information correct? It almost goes without saying that if your data are incorrect your study will be a waste of time and resources. It is also vitally important that the data be accurate because management's decisions for improving the work practices covered by the study will rely on them. To make sure the information is correct and accurate, review it carefully to see if any anomalies stand out. As you give it a simple scan, do you notice any inconsistency in or feel any discomfort about the data? Any reservations you have about the data will have to be resolved! One way to test their veracity is to ask yourself two questions: Are you comfortable with your partner's responses? Did you make any mistakes in recording their responses?

More often than not, the answers to these questions will not make you as sanguine as you want or need to be. In addition, your notes may not be as clear as they seemed when they were taken. In fact, the experience of most benchmarkers suggests that some kind of telephone follow-up is usually necessary. To make your follow-up call most effective, follow these guidelines:

1. Call the person with whom you have the closest relationship.

2. Know specifically what it is you want to clarify, reconcile, or add.

3. Ask specific questions that will provide answers to your missing or incomplete data.

4. Test your understanding about the data with detailed questions such as "What I read the data to say is this. . . . Is that correct?"

Objectives of Phase Three

Once you have completed your reassessment and are satisfied that you have the data you need and that they are accurate, you are ready to proceed with the objective of Phase Three—to diagnose your data while satisfying the requirements of your purpose statement. This is true even if you decide to begin a new study because of incremental information rather than stick with your original plan. You will have accomplished the objectives of Phase Three when you have organized the data; determined if there is a performance gap; described the practice that causes the gap; projected future performance; and avoided the pitfalls of data analysis. These steps are detailed in the balance of this chapter.

Organizing the Data

The first step is to organize the information into a format that will permit evaluation. But before you can assemble it into a form that will allow you to clarify and demonstrate the effects of the practices you have studied, you must be comfortable with it. The best method to organize the data, I believe, is to construct a matrix comparing your partners to one another, process to process. Each process you are evaluating should be broken down into enough detail that it provides a quick overall picture of all the data. This will ensure that all the inconsistencies and exceptions stand out clearly. Camp (1995, p. 145) recommends that the level of detail presented should be decided on by the process owners and the people who do the actual work. To construct such a matrix he offers some guidelines.

1. Set the level of detail low enough so that it is easy to recognize the significant steps in the work process but high enough so that the team does not become mired in unrelated details.

2. Balance the details among the work process steps so that no individual step is weighted more than any of the others.

3. Describe each step in the work process in terms that keep its size small enough to perform a cost analysis.

4. Use a matrix that is easy to understand and clear so that the benchmark leader's performance level stands out as superior to all other partners. This means that the descriptions of the practice and the key summary measures of performance used in the matrix should be easily understood.

Table 4.1 presents such a matrix. Although this examines just one phase of a service training operation, it gives an idea of how benchmarking data can be laid out to provide an overview of the organization's performance outcomes. For the purposes of assessing the process, assume that you are Organization A and that the other five (B through F) are your partners. Which one is better? If "costs per student day" is the important measure, then C, D, E, and F are the better organizations. But if a clearer measure of efficiency is "cost per student," the picture changes. In addition, if you are Organization A, this slice of data might suggest that because of the size of your service training task and the resources you commit to it, you have chosen the wrong partners to study—that you should seek out organizations with smaller training efforts and budgets instead. Also, this view of the data is strictly quantitative. To understand fully its significance, you need to know the qualitative causes behind the numbers.

Table 4.2 offers some of the reasons why the data vary so greatly. Whether or not an organization operates its own facilities and whether it purchases its training or develops it in-house have obvious effects on the numbers. In fact, where at first the numbers may have suggested that you repeat the study with a different set of partners, once the qualitative data are available it becomes apparent that you and Organization D have much in common. You may want to understand its practices better since the performance outcomes are superior. Organization B's data should also be studied in

Table 4.1. Service Training Matrix, Part 1.

	Organization					
	A	B	C	D	E	F
Total operating costs	$300,000	$1,350,000	$2,860,000	$750,000	$3,310,000	$6,350,000
Fixed labor costs	$120,000	$450,000	$850,000	$360,000	$960,000	$1,800,000
Number of classrooms	0	2	3	0	4	10
Number of instructors	1.5	5	10	4	12	20
Annual number of students	200	500	2,000	800	3,000	4,000
Student training days	200	2,500	20,000	4,000	30,000	40,000
Student-instructor ratio	1.5/200	1.5/200	1.5/200	1.5/200	1.5/200	1.5/200
Cost per student	$1,500	$2,700	$1,430	$937	$1,103	$1,587
Cost per student day	$300	$540	$143	$187	$110	$158
Annual student travel costs	0	$400,000	$1,500,000	0	$500,000	$3,000,000
Annual staff travel costs	$20,000	$5,000	$10,000	$40,000	$50,000	$50,000
Number of curriculum developers per instructor	0.3	0.2	0.3	0.12	0.41	0.3
Number of curriculum developers per student	0.0025	0.002	0.0015	0.00062	0.0016	0.0015

Table 4.2. Service Training Matrix, Part 2.

	Organization					
	A	B	C	D	E	F
Develops own training or purchases	Purchases	Develops	Purchases	Purchases	Develops	Develops
Maintains centralized training facility	No[a]	Yes	Yes	No[a]	No[b]	Yes
Maintains training staff	Yes	Yes	Yes	Yes	Yes	Yes
Uses field training	Yes	No	Yes	Yes	Yes	Yes

[a]Uses hotels.
[b]Uses regional facilities.

close detail because the size of its task is not much greater than yours, your costs suggest that you do a better job, and its mode of operating (qualitative measures) is very different.

Expanding Your Study

Perhaps the most common problem for inexperienced benchmarkers during data diagnosis is what is often called "analysis paralysis," that is, getting bogged down in the detail. To avoid analysis paralysis, experienced benchmarkers keep their study's purpose statement on hand while they are conducting the diagnosis. As noted earlier, you may have gathered some really interesting, perhaps even valuable information that is beyond the scope of your original study's plan; it can catch you up like a spider's web. To avoid getting bogged down evaluating information that doesn't pertain to your benchmarking study, you must discipline yourself enough to put it aside for later analysis and study. To do this, you have to keep your eye on your purpose statement.

If you decide to go ahead and take advantage of unplanned data to expand or change your study, you will have to do several things. First, you will have to revise your purpose statement to reflect the new direction. Second, you will have to renegotiate this new plan with your management champion. Third, you will have to consider whether your partners need to be advised of the changes in your study—perhaps even reengaged in some way. Some of the issues to consider are the following:

- Does the unplanned study require you to provide data to your partners that you had not planned to provide?
- Is there a conflict between your original agreement with your partners and the new direction?
- Does the new direction violate any commitments or agreements that you have made to your partners?
- Can you fulfill your obligation to your partners and still pursue the study's new direction?

Keeping Your Study in Focus

Once you have decided on a final strategy for your study and analysis, sort the data based upon your purpose statement, focusing only on the information specifically related to your study. Use simple computations. The best advice any experienced benchmarker can offer a beginner for staying clear of the analysis paralysis trap is to process the data with the intent of being only "roughly" right. Those who have traveled the benchmarking path know to avoid getting bogged down in fine mathematical or statistical detail and simply to reveal which company the data say is best and why. The more experienced people have learned that the purpose of benchmarking is the research of business processes—not genetic DNA forecasts—and that the level of statistical precision between these two is quite different. In fact, all that is needed to tell the story of any benchmarking study successfully is a validated assessment of the information that has been gathered and an interpretation of its meaning. The interpretation should be presented in such a way that the audience will readily understand the data and be willing to depend on it in making decisions about the practices that have been studied. This overview approach is more productive than others. Using statistics extensively isn't always the most effective thing to do—many people have difficulty accepting statistical arguments. Thus, it will serve you well to remember from the very outset of your analysis that the extensive use of statistics frequently suffers because of this general suspicion of statistical tools.

Experience also shows that providing decision makers with an extensive analysis may not be as effective as you might imagine. In today's world senior managers are increasingly challenged to optimize their time; they are forced to be intolerant of masses of data. They are learning to "manage by the facts." In other words, managers are learning to expect that the people performing a particular work process have the capability to evaluate their own results and take action with minimal exposition of the problem to management. John Manoogian, general manager of the Alpha division of Ford Motor Company, put it plainly: "We simply cannot achieve and maintain our goals of leadership in quality, cost, and on-time programs without continuously improving the processes we use to conduct our business" (Rummler and Brache, 1990, p. 115). In an economic climate that puts time at a premium, in order to capitalize on process improvements managers expect work teams to achieve their objectives based on the most quantifiable data available and to present their conclusions and recommendations for process improvements in a clear and crisp fashion, and in a logical sequence. Here is an example of such a presentation:

1. An evaluation of the variations in the work process
2. An evaluation of the alternative solutions to correct the variations
3. The selection of an appropriate solution
4. An evaluation of the effectiveness of the solution's implementation

As was stated earlier, a simple matrix (see again Tables 4.1 and 4.2) is the most powerful way to determine from "roughly right" data if one of your partners is performing better than you are. There are many advantages to such a simple approach but the two most significant are these:

You will avoid attacks on the accuracy of your mathematics. Most people who are not familiar with the benchmarking process have a tendency to disbelieve the results of a study, especially if the news is bad. First, the people directly affected by a study's outcomes will almost certainly want some kind of certification that the results are accurate. Those who might feel threatened by the study will naturally be the most defensive and the most aggressive in reviewing the results. These people are likely to look for cracks in the study's armor and in all probability will be joined by those in the audience whose first inclination is always to challenge anyone else's numbers. To overcome these kinds of objections, you will have to be prepared to explain to them that the purpose of benchmarking is not statistical perfection but the identification of best practices, and the reasons why they exist. At General Motors (GM), CEO Jack Smith has been pushing benchmarking in a big way while at the same time cautioning his organization not to confuse the benchmarking process with "management by numbers." His concern is that at the old GM financial yardsticks were used to measure everything, whether the measurements were meaningful or not (Taylor, 1994). All organizations have lots of people obsessed with numbers because so many have been trained, developed, measured, and motivated in this way throughout their careers. But despite the numerical preferences of your audience, you must remember that by keeping the data simple and in basic, logical format, you increase your chances of thwarting those who may be as quick to pull out their calculators as Wyatt Earp was to draw his .45.

You will avoid getting caught up in proving quantitative rather than qualitative effects. A benchmarking gap is best expressed in quantifiable terms in order to assess the extent of the difference. However, in reality you cannot take any practical action to correct a performance shortfall unless you understand the gap in actionable terms, that is, in words that actually describe the work practice. Once again, managers don't usually think this way. In the course of their day-to-day activities managers are constantly assessing and being assessed by measurements. As a result they are inclined to understand problems in terms of numbers. Yet, getting bogged down in detailing metrics and validating calculations is certain to cloud the understanding of why a number is what it is! As C. J. McNair of Coopers & Lybrand and Kathleen Leibfreid of Babson College say in their book on benchmarking (1992, p. 176), "Traditional corporate scorecards often focus solely on the financial measures or results. There appears to be little recognition that financial results cannot be directly managed but instead are caused by the level of performance on the quality, productivity, and delivery dimensions." The *Los Angeles Times* (Flanigan, 1995, p. D3) reported that "conventional statistics have not captured the changes occurring this decade in the U.S. economy" when they noted that the growth of productivity was diagnosed for a long time as a jobless recovery, until UCLA's Anderson School of Management reported that in recent years both jobs and wages had grown along with efficiency. As the *Times* reported, the economy was not really the problem. Instead, understanding of it was flawed because traditional, purely statistical measures did not account for the increase in nontraditional information-based jobs.

The actual process of diagnosing the data includes two interrelated steps: *tabulating the data* and *analyzing the data*.

Tabulating the Data

Tabulating the data begins with a review of all the information you have acquired to ensure that it is complete and consistent with all the questions that were asked during the data-gathering process, whether in mail surveys, telephone interviews, or site visits. As already suggested, it is best to keep your calculations to simple computations, including averages, percentages, and minimum and maximum values. In this way, you can tell your story in the clearest way possible. Also, by having your information in a format that allows for easy evaluation, such as histograms and Pareto charts (the seven statistical tools of quality) and pie charts, you will improve your chances of avoiding conflict. Remember, too, to synthesize the qualitative data and capture the key messages from these sources in a meaningful format.

Keep tabulation and formatting processes simple and to the point by answering questions like these: What do the data say? Are the differences in the performance measures clear? How large are the gaps?

As this point, you may want to consider the advantages of a statistician's services. There is no question that a statistician can be extremely helpful in assisting you to understand the data and prepare graphics that will tell your study's story in the most effective way. A word of caution, however. It is wise not to let a statistician take total control of tabulating and displaying your data. *Remain involved.* Statisticians who have not been involved with the study from the beginning may construct the information in such a way that the data portray a story you have not heard before. Or they may display the information in such a way that you aren't able to interpret it. Either way, you won't be able to explain your study and present conclusions to your audience. Wise benchmarkers agree that if you wish to champion a plan of corrective action, there is no way to avoid intimacy with your data.

A story about Winston Churchill illustrates the point well. During World War II, Churchill asked a general to plan the logistics for a battle. The general said he doubted he should be involved in such technical matters because, "You know, they say familiarity breeds contempt." To that, Churchill reportedly responded, "I would like to remind you that without a degree of familiarity, we could not breed anything." This is why the benchmarking team members must always have the capacity to understand and interpret the data they have collected, no matter how much support they receive from others.

Analyzing the Data

Begin the analysis of a benchmarking study's results by separating out those statistics that are not related to the original purpose. (Incidentally, this is another good way to revalidate the purpose statement.) Second, make certain that the metrics you are using are only "roughly right." Remember, this generalist approach might seem to be contradictory to your purpose but it is actually important to your success. Guard against being overly precise. Most experienced benchmarkers would agree that two decimals are more than sufficient for adequate presentation of the measures of your findings.

However, just keeping the numbers simple is not enough. To make a thorough analysis, you must be aware of the industrial, economic, cultural, and other environmental factors in which your organization operates. So don't forget all the anecdotal information you acquired. The "war stories" and personal experiences provide a fertile ground of insight and revelation regarding the causes for the gaps in performance between organizations. However, while you always want to be open for key messages in these anecdotal explanations, you also want to avoid merely stating the obvious. The most important thing to keep in mind is to synthesize the key points into a few easy to understand statements. A simple review of the responses to each question you asked should provide you an idea of the best way to lay out the narrative.

The objective of the data analysis is to help the team members draw conclusions about what they heard and saw and to facilitate their assessment of what they have learned. To do this effectively you must understand that the data will suggest different things to different members of the team. Remember, your partners responded based on their own culture, vision, challenges, and other factors and forces unique to their enterprises. In turn, your team members listened based on their own culture, vision, challenges, and other factors and forces that are unique to your enterprise. While your benchmarking team may have hoped to uncover quick or easy opportunities for improvements during the earlier steps in the benchmarking process, at this stage they must examine a broad array of information in order to discover new ways of organizing their work and work flows. This may sound complex but, nevertheless, if the team's analysis is thorough and accurate, at the end of the study the team will be prepared to make recommendations for an action plan that should offer opportunities to substantially improve their work process (McNair and Leibfreid, 1992).

Determining If There Is a Gap

The delta between your performance level and that of the benchmark organization is commonly known as "the gap." Once you determine the gap between your own performance and that of the benchmarking leader, you can learn what you have to do to improve your performance. After a gap has been identified, its analysis will help you uncover the root causes. Peeling back each layer until the root cause is clear will reveal the best practices that hold the key to your closing the gap between you and the benchmarking leader.

It is quite easy to identify a performance gap. Once you have made sure of the consistency between your internal data and the data collected from your partners—in other words, once you have separated your partner's apples from your oranges (and vice versa)—you should have no difficulty in clearly identifying which partner is the leader and in comparing your own measurement data against that of the benchmark organization.

Illustration of the gap may be accomplished by a simple formula:

$$\text{Gap} = \text{internal measurement} - \text{benchmark}$$

The outcome of this formula will indicate one of three types of performance gaps. A *negative gap* exists when a partner's practice is clearly superior to your own. You are at *parity* when there is no appreciable, or discernable, difference between you and your partner's performance level; there is no gap, therefore it can be said that both organizations are equal or at parity with one another. A *positive gap* exists when you are the benchmark because by all the measures your practices are superior.

Negative Gaps

A negative gap exists when the benchmark organization is your partner. Most significant, this gap signals that if your organization is to challenge or exceed the metrics of the benchmarking leader then you will have to be prepared to mobilize a major effort to make changes to your internal practices and methods. In order to make such changes your analysis must focus on understanding why the differences exist and what specific changes will be needed in order to close the gap. Practices like these will lead to the improvements that will eventually result in your achieving a competitive edge. Although at first a negative gap may seem overwhelming, experience shows that the real secret to success in changing the direction of an organization is incremental improvements. Quantum leaps may seem great but they are infrequent and sometimes have disruptive "whirlwind" effects on organizations. In contrast, small improvements build upon themselves as one success leads to another, and a positive pattern of improvement, high expectations, and growth in confidence result. Of course, always keep in mind that most success stories take many years. Xerox launched its drive to total quality management with its first benchmarking study in 1979. It won the Malcolm Baldrige Quality Award ten years later.

Parity

Two benchmarking organizations are at parity when there is no significant differences in the methods that they are using. When a benchmarking study provides this result, there is sometimes a tendency to think of the state of affairs as "a tie." Indeed, this is somewhat true because although there may be slight differences in methods between the two organizations, despite these different ways of doing things the outcomes, or results, are essentially the same. That said, there are nevertheless dangers in thinking about parity as a tie because it leads to complacency. A tie suggests that the competition has ended, that your partner is picking up the ball, ending the game, and going home; but in the competitive world of the industrial economy this is not very likely. Also, a tie game is often considered a disappointment (remember the old saw, "a tie is like kissing your sister"), as though it hadn't been worth playing.

To guard against such thinking, an organization that is at parity with its partners it should be especially alert to all the factors that contributed to this situation. This is especially important for an organization that wants to gain superiority because superior organizations are always striving to discover new work process methods that will eventually lead to their being the positive benchmark. Such organizations never see parity as a form of "kissing their sister" because they see competition as both a challenge and an opportunity. They avoid getting caught resting on their laurels because they emphasize the admonitions that most total quality organizations make to their employees: "Are we doing the right things? And even if we are, are we doing these things right?" To be sure your organization is both doing the right things and doing them right, you should consider the following questions: Are your operations performing their methods in the right way? Are these operations using the most efficient methods available? Are they performing the right methods? Are the work methods installed effectively?

Positive Gaps

A positive gap exists between you and your partners when the measurement of your organization's performance is clearly superior to the measurement of your partner's performance. This means that you are the benchmark organization. When this is the case there are three important things for you to think about. First, are you exacting an unnecessary cost for being the benchmark leader? To make this determination, think about your definition of quality. If you accept that the definition of quality is to meet your customers' requirements, then are you exceeding those requirements unnecessarily? As James Donlon, Chrysler's controller, says, "Just because somebody has been very successful with an order-to-delivery cycle of twenty-five days doesn't mean that your cycle should be twenty-five days also, even if you're in the same industry" (Ozanian, 1993, p. 53).

Second, be aware that there will most likely be a level of skepticism within your organization about your operation being truly superior to your partners. In most organizations there is a sort of cognitive consonance that teaches us that in order to be successful we must always try harder. At the same time, because we are so achievement-oriented, whenever people try to gain acknowledgment that their goals have been met and success achieved, a cognitive dissonance emerges to say we should be suspicious. It is likely that this mentality stems from the attitude that all our objectives are stretch targets, that is, we don't really expect to meet the target, but in case we do, it wasn't high enough! In time, we hope, benchmarking will bring a measure of reality to goal setting. But until that happens in your organization, it is smart to remember that if your organization is committed to the strategy of constantly raising the performance bar regardless of what the performance measures actually say, then the burden of proof of the quality of your benchmarking data will be on you.

Finally, when you are the benchmark organization—even if it is a subordinate function that is in question—you will have to learn to blow your own horn loudly and clearly. The reason for this is not to stroke your own ego but to advance the cause of benchmarking. Broadcasting your success story throughout the organization provides recognition not only to your team and management champion but also to the benchmarking process itself. Even more important, by giving your accomplishments and performance leadership extensive visibility and getting recognition throughout the organization, you will motivate others to close any negative gaps that might exist elsewhere in the organization. Your example will encourage others to master benchmarking as a performance improvement tool.

Describing the Practice That Causes the Gap

As already mentioned, people generally tend to state the quantitative aspects of an issue before fully understanding the qualitative factors. Perhaps this is so because it allows them to express their opinions first, while they are unencumbered by the facts; this is a practice that we human beings seem to enjoy. In benchmarking, however, this can be a serious problem. Experience shows that concentrating on the quantitative as the motive for a benchmarking study to the exclusion of the qualitative is a grave mistake. After you have conducted benchmarking studies for a few years, I believe you too will always want to give the qualitative precedence in your benchmarking analysis. You will learn that the qualitative assessment is the one that explains why a metric is what it is; that the qualitative description explains to management the real reason for the difference between benchmarking leader and partners. Only when the reasons behind the organizations' different practices are absolutely clear will the analytical measure—the metric that shows the size of the difference—be understandable.

Although a qualitative narrative describes the best practice and the opportunity for improvement, the quantitative description measures the size of the gap and thus reveals the scope of the improvement opportunity. Here is an example statement: "The benchmark organization has a more proficient service training function. Therefore, their cost per student day is $20 less than ours."

A qualitative definition is a narrative description of the practice that you benchmarked and the conclusions you reached based on your analysis of the data. It should also include an observation of the opportunity for improvement based on what you have learned. Therefore, your description should not stop with *what is* but go beyond a cursory assessment to describe the *why* and the *how* of the improvement opportunity that the gap in practices presents to your organization.

Once the gap is known and has been expressed in a way that it is easily understandable to people familiar with the work process, the next step in diagnosing the data is to identify exactly why the benchmark organization is better. What is at first apparent is not always the complete answer; there is usually more than one reason why an organization is more effective than another. Understanding what the possible causes are, why they exist, and how they work is important if you wish to know which actions should be taken to improve your own practices. If your data gathering has been effective, you will have learned the root causes for the gap and obtained the key information you need to support your findings.

It should be noted that if you do not understand the root causes for a partner's superiority by this point in your analysis then you should question the reliability of your results. Although the reasons you use to prove why the gap exists do not have to be quantifiable they do have to be *directionally correct*. For example, Motorola's well-known Six Sigma program for the reduction of its product defect and error rates was adopted without any specific tactical operational plans. In fact, Motorola management recognized that Six Sigma would represent stretch goals that would challenge the entire organization. This meant that even though there were only five thousand defective items out of a million (99.5 percent were good), they would strive to reduce that rate by one-tenth or produce only five hundred defective items out of a million. Management knew that this goal needed to be achieved if Motorola was to be recognized for world-class products. But management also knew that achieving such goals would require that the organization work smarter, not just harder. To accomplish this Motorola "began soliciting new ideas and benchmarking their competitors to determine yardsticks to measure their performance" (Denton, 1991, p. 23). An interesting point here is that people benchmarking Motorola during this time would have been misled unless they knew that the key driver of Motorola's new measurement criteria was to raise performance expectations.

Because it provides an insight into your opportunities for improvement, the written statement explaining the gap is the core benefit of your benchmarking effort. Therefore, the strategic implications of your gap analysis statement can't be treated lightly. Your written statement provides the documentation and impetus for change, for adapting the best practice.

Thus, an example of a more complete analysis statement is the following: "The cost gap of $20 per student day between us and the benchmark leader is due to lower instructor salaries (in the range of 10 percent to 15 percent) and a higher ratio of instructors to students (1:30 versus 1:20)."

Drivers of the Gap

So far we have established that the purpose of benchmarking is to learn how your operations stack up against your partners, what differences there might be in your comparable practices, and what the size of any gaps that exist between you and the benchmark leader is. By itself this knowledge can only be a frame of reference. Just knowing that a gap exists and why it exists is not enough because deciding what actions you will have to take to correct a problem means that you fully understand the reasons why there is a gap. During your data gathering, it is hoped that you paid attention to the conditions within and the strategies employed by your partner organizations. If you listened carefully to what was being said, kept your eyes open during the site visits, and asked *why* whenever something wasn't clear, then you will have a good sense of your partners' operations. If you have done these things you will probably know the answers to these questions: Why do they do things the way they do them? What investments have they made to improve their work processes? What do they regard as more important to provide the customer—volume or value? Is employee empowerment important to them; that is, do they embrace the principles of total quality management or are they autocratic? What does your intuition say about their operations?

The answers to these questions will give you real insight into the root causes of the benchmarking leader's success. However, you also should remember that most organizational drivers are subtle factors. They are not always apparent to the casual observer. For example, an organization has been judged to possess a highly productive engineering staff as measured, let's say, by drawings per engineer. This organization may have achieved its productivity by making investments in engineering support tools like workstations and CAD software. However, maybe another organization across the street achieved the same productivity measures by requiring its engineering staff to work more hours than others do. And further down the street, perhaps yet another organization has achieved even greater efficiency by providing the staff with unusually profitable incentives to increase outputs. Thus, an analysis of the metrics alone would be very misleading in determining which organization is truly the leader.

What You Should Consider

If your study has been comprehensive, then you should pretty much know why the benchmark is in fact superior. In other words, based on the results of the study, you should know what is driving the benchmark leader's superior performance. To verify what the driver might be, take the following items into consideration.

Business Practices. Are there any new or unique work processes that the leader might be using (that is, Motorola's Six Sigma program and Xerox's Leadership Through Quality)?

Work Standards. How does the benchmarking leader measure performance and productivity? Does it measure the same things that the other partners do, and in the same way?

Work Environment. Is there anything unique about this organization's facilities, tools, or management processes? Does its uniqueness provide it any special advantage over partners?

Economics. Is there anything going on in that firm's industry that requires it to behave differently than your own organization? For example, perhaps its marketplace has become saturated, requiring competitors to decrease operating expenses. If the benchmarking leader is foreign-owned or has a strong foreign partner, is there anything going on in that country's economy that provides an advantage? Does anything require it to behave differently than your own organization?

Culture. An organization's behavior and performance will always be affected by the national culture of its employees. Therefore national culture should be considered during the benchmarking study. But a benchmarking team should not lose sight of the organization's own culture—regardless of its nationality—because historically what a company values and what it rewards will be the strongest determinants of the organization's behavior.

There is no better example of understanding the impact of culture than a recent experience of the Japanese and Koreans, who were managing their share of the *maquiladoras*, the foreign-owned plants that were set up in Baja, Mexico, to take advantage of that country's low-cost labor. The Japanese, who arrived in Mexico in the 1980s, learned their own work culture and standards, which they had imposed at other facilities worldwide, would not be accepted here. High turnover taught them that neither their traditional prework exercise programs nor employee uniforms would be accepted and that Mexican workers, who value family before work, would bristle and walk away from even well-paying jobs if there was frequent, unscheduled overtime. Sony bemoaned the fact that many employees did not return to work after the Christmas holidays, but when it found that many of the absentees were workers who went to the interior of Mexico for the holidays, it solved the problem by hiring buses to bring the workers back. The Koreans, who followed the Japanese in the *maquiladoras*, learned that Mexican workers want to take time off to pay their rent or take care of civil obligations. For example, Hitachi's workers grumbled about working Thursday and Friday of Holy Week. Nonetheless they showed up for work on a day that most Mexicans had off after cultural sensitivity and communications between employees and their Korean employer increased. The importance of such communications efforts is also working at other Korean companies. Although average turnover for *maquiladoras* is 8 percent, Hyundai has lowered its monthly employee turnover from 20 percent two years ago to 5 percent in 1995 (Kraul and Iritani, 1995).

In 1989–1990, SRI International conducted a study for Shell Oil Company's downstream operations to identify the effectiveness of its technical support delivery. The premise was that the right technology had to be delivered to the right place at the right time. SRI knew that it is necessary to understand that "the implications for technology response and support are broad, affecting every function and every business activity" (Colmen, 1993, p. 32). Significantly, SRI discovered that performance profiles varied by geography and industry. For example, Japanese companies were better than average in every category except information technology use while U.S. companies led in information technology use and human resources. Meanwhile, European participants excelled in adaptability to change, that is, recognizing the need to change, being willing to change, and effectively implementing change. What is interesting is that not many years ago European companies would have fared less well, but the Single European Act has become a powerful driver of change (Colmen, 1993, p. 34). Since the study was conducted, the opening of Eastern Europe has provided an added impetus for adapting to a changing environment and events have shown that, from an industry point of view, the more dynamic the role of technology and the more frequent the demand for product and process change, the better the technical support delivery performance (Colmen, 1993). Obviously, culture had a significant effect on the outcome of the study.

Incidentally, some of the best practices that SRI discovered were the following:

- Having active commitment on the part of top management in good times and bad
- Ensuring that employees were aware of the organization's strategy and direction and especially of change
- Paying special attention to long-term technical needs
- Taking management risks in order to be first to market
- Decentralizing information technology functions

- Using external technical resources extensively to complement and supplement internal resources
- Anticipating environmental requirements and upgrading processes for competitive advantage

Projecting Future Performance

Once you understand why a gap exists, the next point to consider is its long-term effect. You must attempt to anticipate if the gap will decrease or increase over time. The answer to this question can only be found by projecting the gap based on probable future performance and trends. It is important to do this because in today's competitive world when all organizations are pursuing productivity improvements, it is unlikely that benchmark organizations will sit on their laurels. Nothing in this world remains static; everything is in constant change. Organizations everywhere—both private and public—are increasingly conscious of productivity and they know they cannot expect their competitors to wait for them to catch up. For this reason, while actually gathering data from your partners it is wise to keep in mind that you will have to use that data to make projections of your partner's future performance levels.

Both Camp and Spendolini point out the importance of projecting trends and a future gap because industry practices are constantly changing. They both stress that the principal value of such projections is to help define the goals and targets you will have to achieve in order to close the gap. Benchmarking experts advocate projecting out three to five years depending on historical productivity trends, the size of the gap, and what people closest to the work expect their future productivity to be. The trends that should be used are those that you can clearly observe. They are usually stated as a percentage. For example, "Currently our organization has a 5 percent gap against the benchmark organization in product quality. However, industry trends show an improvement of 1 percent per year in the benchmark leader's performance. Therefore, we project the gap will be 10 percent in five years unless corrective action is taken."

Making this kind of projection is not as difficult as it may sound. In fact, if you know the reasons for the gap, have some knowledge of the benchmarking leader's past trends, and have identified its drivers, then you have everything you need to make a reliable projection.

Determining the Trends

It is commonly known that organizations that lead do not sit still. Because they aim for moving targets, organizations that wish to lead must learn to overshoot their goals, raise their expectations. As Dave Kearns (Kearns and Nadler, 1992, p. 125) said of Xerox, "We don't expect enough of ourselves." So it was with the SRI study for Shell Oil. The study concluded that in vying for leadership an organization must learn to overshoot. The study noted, "The leading company has cut back in some programs that contributed to its prominence. It was a question of cost/value trade-offs. How good do you have to be as a leader? Is it worth getting too far ahead of the pack? What happens, however, if you stop watching your competitors? Might you hear footsteps?" (Colmen, 1993, p. 35).

It is very difficult to project a gap without at least some historical productivity data or performance measures for both your organization and the benchmarking leader. The results of your study are, of course, just a snapshot—a moment in time, so to speak. But when you add data from your industry and your organization to your benchmarking subject's database, trends invariably start to emerge and become clear. With data for more than one year for both your company and the benchmarking leader, trends are more easily discernible.

If you have no historical data you will have to resort to *guestimates*, that is, your best estimates of what the benchmark levels and your performance will be in three to five years. Base your guestimates on your knowledge of the plans and goals of the benchmark leader and of your own operation, projecting both companies' performance over the same period of years. You can also use industry or professional databases such as those available from the Chamber of Commerce, the Bureau of National Affairs, the Commerce Clearing House, and the American Productivity and Quality Center in Houston. In addition, many trade and professional associations, as well as state and federal government bureaus, can provide annual productivity reports and forecasts.

Finally, determine if the gap is widening or closing, then estimate the size of the gap over the next several years. Such forecasts are best depicted in graphs. Remember, it is on the basis of these forecasts that your organization will select the most promising tactical or strategic plans for closing the gap.

The Z Chart

To visualize the effect of future trends and decisions, a graphic tool should demonstrate the three essential components: current gap size, historical productivity trends, and projected future gap. The best tool developed so far to accomplish these objectives is the Z Chart. (See Figure 4.1.) The Z Chart is a graph that portrays a benchmark leader's measure against your own—or as Fitz-enz notes (1993, p. 31), it "shows the score plainly and objectively." A Z Chart calibrates the size of a gap, shows how it might change in the future, and shows the future trends both with and without corrective action. To make it easy for people to read the story of the data, a Z Chart should be based on a single summary statistic, one that portrays the function's or the organization's overall performance.

A word of caution is again necessary here. Although benchmarking is more useful than competitive analysis in clarifying competitor movements and trends, a benchmarking study has its own limitations. The purpose is to understand current best practices in order to improve your own performance. To apply linear thinking to what you have learned for the purpose of projecting goals is

Figure 4.1. The Z Chart.

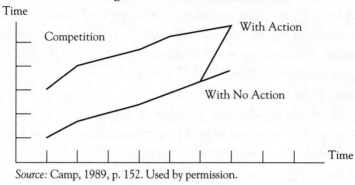

Source: Camp, 1989, p. 152. Used by permission.

dangerous because behavior in the real world often isn't linear. Projections of future potential rarely follow the historical model. As Greg Watson (1992, pp. 81–82) advises, "Any goal that you set should be tested for reasonability."

A good way to optimize use of a Z Chart is to analyze the data in terms of three categories:

Tactical Actions. Historically, real gains in productivity have been achieved through gradual, deliberate tactical changes to an organization's processes. Tactical actions are taken to achieve an objective that has been planned to be accomplished in one to two years. A tactical plan usually consists of a series of tasks that represent a specific course of action to meet the objective—the tactical plan is the "how" while the objective is the "what." Both represent specific, measurable intents on the part of management. These kind of improvements are driven by internal observations of the work process and are based upon the experience and knowledge of the people doing the work. By implementing these kinds of tactical actions management usually expects to achieve productivity improvements of up to 5 percent.

Strategic Actions. When a benchmarking partner's leadership has been achieved by an industry-leading best practice, it is most often the result of strategic planning. Overcoming a performance leader's superiority that is the result of strategic decisions usually requires strategic action. The intent of a strategic plan is broader than tactical actions. It is therefore most commonly a wide course of action aimed at attaining an organizational goal. Organizational goals are what the organization expects to attain through a sustained effort over a long period of time. Supporting such goals requires a plan of action that invariably has been chosen from a number of alternative actions and will take a minimum of two years to accomplish.

Extent of the Gap. Understanding the full extent of any gap is often revealing and a sobering experience. Once past that feeling, there is usually the hope that one major practice change can close the gap; that with one single, masterful stroke all will be well. The truth, however, is that superior performance is the result of constant attention to structured, planned changes, implemented with knowledge of what is to be done and how it will be done, within a framework that informs you when you have succeeded. Patience is the watchword here—patience to restrain the organization, especially managers, from rash action, because once the full extent of the gap is known only an equally extensive plan will correct the problem.

David Sheffield, vice president of finance for Janssen Pharmaceutica (a subsidiary of Johnson & Johnson) said: "I've found that having these data doesn't automatically lead to doing anything with them; they can make you happy or sad but not much smarter. You can't immediately go after the areas where you need to improve, because you don't know how the other companies work. If you are going to go through the benchmarking effort you have to remember that it's only a starting point. You need to do something with the information once you get it" (McNair and Leibfreid, 1992, p. 139).

Avoiding the Pitfalls of Data Analysis

As we have noted throughout this chapter there are many potential pitfalls that you will want to avoid when you are interpreting your data and laying the groundwork for action planning.

Although I have already commented on each of them, a few reminders can't hurt.

Analysis Paralysis

Unless you keep your assessment of the data "roughly right" and avoid overprecision, it is likely that you will overanalyze the information you have gathered, lose your direction, and leave yourself open to criticism from the nitpickers who are inevitably in every audience.

Wandering from Your Purpose

Without constant referral to your purpose statement you are likely to be led by the extent of the information you have gathered into areas not approved for your study. Although you may gather information that is salient to your organization, unless it is part of your original purpose, it may be best to set it aside for another time.

Being Closed to Cause and Effect

Many things are not as they first appear. The reasons you believe to be behind the problem may not survive the test of cause and effect. Unless you are able to make the connection between the problem and its cause, you haven't captured the true root cause and will not be able to craft a successful, enduring solution.

Misunderstanding the Reasons for the Gap

Whether you use cause-and-effect analysis or look at the drivers behind the benchmarking leader's performance, if you do not know why the performance gap between you and the leader exists, you will not be able to develop an effective strategy of corrective action.

Missing Drivers and Enabling Practices

The reasons for an organization's success are often rooted in motivations that are not at first apparent or that may not even be specifically related to the metric. The drive for productivity, leadership, or excellence is often the result not of specific management decisions but of unrelated factors. Unless these drivers are correctly identified, efforts to close the performance gap are likely to fail.

Ignoring the Gap

Unless you project the performance of both your organization and the benchmarking leader it will be virtually impossible for you to identify a corrective action plan that is focused beyond the here and now. Without a reasonable forecast upon which to overlay planning, you will have difficulty both knowing how to craft your corrective action plan and deciding how great an investment you should make.

Avoiding or overcoming these pitfalls is essential to the successful interpretation of the data you have gathered. You need a clear idea of the problem you face and why your benchmarking partner has been more successful than you have in order to establish a best practice of your own.

Concluding Thoughts

Phase Three's objective is twofold: to take advantage of the information your partners have shared with you and to understand better the significance of the information you gathered about your own organization during Phase Two. Once you have accomplished both of these things you will have learned some things that can begin to build your confidence. When you possess knowledge about your own strengths and weaknesses and those of organizations you respect you may avoid being "vulnerable to the valor of ignorance," as George Patton put it (Toland, 1991, p. 99). You are also ready to make use of what you have learned.

Chapter Five

Phase Four

Internalizing the Results and Closing the Gap with the Competition

> There aren't any great men. There are just great
> challenges that ordinary men like you and me are
> forced by circumstances to meet.
> —*Admiral William F. Halsey*

In their widely acclaimed book *The Leadership Challenge*, James Kouzes and Barry Posner (1987, p. 113) wrote: "No matter how grand the dream of the individual visionary, if others do not see in it the possibility of realizing their own hopes and desires, they will not follow. It is incumbent upon the leader to show others how they too will be served by the long-term vision of the future." The following is an example.

Within six months of joining Chrysler Corporation, Lee Iacocca had learned how encumbered with unprofitable operations, debilitating business practices, and misplaced executives his new corporation had become. By November 1978 he knew that he was the captain of a sinking ship and that he would have to do much more than simply rearrange the deck chairs.

In his autobiography, Iacocca (Iacocca and Novak, 1984, pp. 229–266) tells the story of Chrysler's escape from bankruptcy. Once he understood the extent of the problem and formulated ideas on how the company could be rescued, Iacocca recruited a management team that shared his faith in the plan. Together they set about reducing overhead, streamlining business processes, and closing or selling operations, including a profitable tank division that was acquired by General Dynamics for $348 million. But Chrysler needed billions. Thus there were loans and loan guarantees from the U.S. government and concessions from Chrysler employees. The Chrysler management team had the facts and they believed they had the plan to correct the problems, but first they had to sell their recovery plan to Congress, the financial community, Chrysler employees, the United Auto Workers (UAW), suppliers, distributors, and the American public. Then they would have to implement their plan and make their dream of a successful Chrysler a reality. Chrysler's data were sound, its plans believable, and its communications plan comprehensive and credible. A prosperous Chrysler today is testimony to how effective Iacocca and his management team were in selling their ideas and then making them happen.

Purpose of Phase Four

There is an old adage to which not enough managers give serious thought: "If we don't change direction, we just may end up where we're headed."

The purpose of this fourth and final phase of the benchmarking process is for the organization to internalize thoroughly the benchmarking study's results and launch action plans that will close the performance gaps with the benchmarking leaders. Simply stated, the purpose is to identify which of the organization's goals need to be changed and to have confidence that the new direction is communicated effectively.

However, before any change can be implemented in your organization, you will have to discern who has to know the specifics of the plan for making the required changes. You and the others who will implement the action plan will also need to agree on how progress to the new goals will be monitored. You will have to make a plan for "recalibrating" the study with your partners.

Objectives of Phase Four

Phase Four has four objectives: communicating the benchmarking findings; integrating the study results into business operations; taking action to close the gaps; and monitoring the implementation of the plan. This chapter explains how you can attain these four objectives.

Communicating the Benchmark Findings

There is much more to communicating the results of a benchmarking study than first meets the eye. Successful communication is more than a simple presentation of the results or your recommendations. The first task is to be certain that your management champion has seen the results, agrees with the proposed actions, and will actively support them. It also means engaging all the people who will be affected by the study's outcomes to determine if they will support them or oppose them. It is particularly important to gain the concurrence of those who must approve or implement the action plan you propose. However, before presenting the study and your recommendations, you must review the organization's current goals to determine what changes will have to be made. Your objective is to guarantee that when the communication takes place there will be unanimous support for the actions you propose. As Spendolini (1992, p. 181) says, "There should be few surprises as you reach the end of the benchmarking process."

Although a communications plan should be focused on overcoming any reluctance stakeholders might have in accepting the study's findings, this is no easy task. Opening people's minds to new ideas almost always produces conflict. It isn't realistic to expect to shift old cultures, habits, ideas, and practices without some resistance. This kind of resistance can be overcome if the communications strategy is built around three key elements: the audience for the study and the implications of your recommendations on them;

the methods of communication you choose to utilize; the way in which you organize and present your analysis.

The Audience

A communications strategy presumes that there is a message to be conveyed and an audience to receive it. But any communications strategy that hopes to succeed must accurately comprehend its audience and what that audience needs to know. To begin with, you have to understand exactly which people should be included in the audience, what their expectations might be, and most important, how the study will specifically affect them. Keep in mind that by the term *audience* I mean those who will receive the message, regardless of the medium, and not merely those attending a presentation. In identifying the people who should compose the audience, think of all the levels within the organization that will be affected by the proposed changes in work practices and the people who will be directly responsible for meeting the new performance standards. Of course, management has to be included because unless management knows the basis for the new benchmarks it won't buy into the rationale. Without that buy in, the support that is necessary to implement the study's changes will not be available. Similarly, if those employees whose work processes will change were not involved with the study, they need to be sold on the value of the new work methods; if not, they will not be a very happy audience. Suppliers also may feel the effects of the recommendations and if they have not already participated they should be engaged early on. If customers are directly affected by such changes as those relating to a billing system or customer service processes, then great care will have to be taken in how they are to be advised. Later in this chapter I'll talk specifically about how action plans that affect customers should be implemented.

Assume that your audience will include some skeptics. This is especially likely among people who have not had some kind of contact with the marketplace and work environment outside the organization. (We will cover gaining acceptance for the study and the action plan later in this chapter.) It is important to note that overcoming resistance to a study and its results will require a comprehensive communications approach. A good example of the value of this kind of preparation is the recent transformation of Hewlett-Packard's Test and Measurement Organization (TMO) from basic microwave instrumentation products to the video business (Groves, 1995, p. D6). As the oldest division in HP, such a break with the past was threatening to TMO's employees. But management was effective in communicating a compelling vision for TMO's future. Employees became excited about the change. Management crafted a strategy to instill enthusiasm in a skeptical work force by regular face-to-face conversations called "coffee talks" and held numerous "hallway chats" to discuss the vision, facilitating employee conversations with customers both old and new. Today the division produces video servers designed for such interactive technologies as movies on demand and has entered a joint venture with Oracle to provide interactive TV equipment for Pacific Telesis. Rather than fearing change, management's communication strategy has TMO's employees embracing it.

Methods of Communicating

Once the people in your organization who are most affected by the findings become aware of your study, they will want to know exactly where they stand and what will be expected of them. Because both their work processes and the measures used to guide or evaluate their performance could change or become unclear to them, these people are likely to take rumor for fact and then try to modify and adapt these rumors into workable and actionable plans for themselves. The problem is that the plans they make may not be what you have in mind. When you come to them to elicit their support, you will likely find some well-entrenched opposition. This is why the paramount objective of your communications strategy should be to overcome resistance to the study and gain acceptance for its findings. For these reasons, the makeup of your audience will be the single most influential factor in deciding which methods of communications to choose, regardless of whether they are written reports, a newsletter on benchmarking, or formal presentations.

Written Reports. Keeping your people advised about the study's progress through the first three phases will go a long way to ensuring that no one is surprised by its results. There are two simple tools you can use to accomplish this: *progress reports* and *trip reports*. A basic written report—a progress report—summarizing the benchmarking team's findings from Phase One to the present can be an effective means of communicating your progress and gaining the organization's support. After this basic report is issued, it can then be updated and republished as you progress. In this way your audience will remain advised of your discoveries while you can influence how they feel about the changes that will have to be employed. Trip reports are another way to keep your audience updated. Somewhat more limited than progress reports because they describe only one or two site visits, they are a timely way to communicate specific findings. Teams often dislike preparing trip reports because of the added work involved, but there is a distinct added value from such reports—the early documenting and communicating of the key data you have uncovered. The work load associated with trip reports can be eased by documenting the team's debriefing session in some detail and then translating it into the trip report. A summary of several trip reports can also be used to form an effective, comprehensive report on your findings (Camp, 1989, p. 165). A final written report should of course accompany your presentation to senior management. (We'll discuss this in more detail later.)

Newsletters. A newsletter is an excellent tool for reaching a large audience. Although the idea of a newsletter may seem a bit overwhelming to some, such a communications vehicle need not be elaborate. All that is necessary is a regularly published, broadly distributed document that promotes the understanding of bench-marking and aims to build support for the use and improvement of benchmarking in your organization. The goal is to promote the use of best practices in your products, services, and business processes by showcasing your benchmarking efforts, providing contacts for consulting, training, and materials, and setting expectations for benchmarking excellence. One way to accomplish this goal is to structure the newsletter around internal case examples of bench-marking successes and articles about other organizations' bench-marking studies. These are powerful ways to reinforce your message and to demonstrate benchmarking competency. A newsletter may also ensure the linkage of benchmarking to the organization's goals and planning processes by conveying real stories of how bench-marking has led to organization objectives. It may also contain requests for benchmarking study participation from both inside and outside the organization.

Formal Presentations. Regardless of whether you use written reports or a newsletter, some formal presentations will very proba-bly be necessary. At the very least reviews have to be conducted with the affected organizations. If you have followed through in the first three phases in a disciplined manner, you should have a sound, credible base upon which to present your data and gain acceptance for its findings. But remember, you want to avoid surprises, espe-cially in a public forum. It is always advisable to meet with senior managers and small groups of the employees most directly affected by the study in one-on-one sessions before any public review. In other words, let them see and touch the data before they are pre-sented to their superiors, peers, and subordinates. This will give them an opportunity to influence the format and the final recom-mendations—to take some ownership—and will go a long way in ensuring their support. Fitz-enz (1993, p. 156) recommends also giving serious consideration to the site of the presentation because the atmosphere can add to or detract from your purpose. He tries to hold his feedback sessions "in a space that lets people feel comfortable and receptive." Experienced benchmarkers would agree that the time you spend planning both the site and the presentation will more than pay for itself in your audience's response.

Organization of the Analysis

A benchmarking team cannot prepare an executive report or presentation within a vacuum. Rather, the team has to work with both senior management and the owners of the work processes that have been studied in order to reach agreement on the content of the presentation. In particular, consensus must be reached in the following areas.

Key Findings. What did the team learn from the study? Are you, or is one of your partners, the benchmark organization? If there is a performance gap between you and a partner, how great is it and what are the key drivers causing it? You want to answer these questions in as concise but expressive a manner as possible so that your audience will readily understand what the study and your data analysis have revealed. The answers are best displayed in terms and metrics with which the audience is familiar. For example, the results of a service training study might be put this way: "Partner A's cost per student day is $20 less than ours, because the instructor salaries are 10 percent to 15 percent less, and their instructor-to-student ratio is better than ours by ten students (1:30 versus 1:20)."

Ranking the Recommendations. How do you propose to correct the performance problems that you have found? Your recommendations must be directly linked to the problems to be corrected and stated unequivocally. But because your findings are certain to suggest more than one appropriate action, it is wise to rank your team's suggestions. For one thing, some issues are likely to be more critical than others. The criticality of some proposals may be so great that their importance exceeds the other recommendations, requiring that management focus on those priorities alone. Another reason for ranking recommendations is that it is likely that the organization will not able to act on everything you propose. In fact, it is rare that an organization is able to do everything that it wants or needs to do simply because of resource constraints. Although a set of actions may at first appear to be quite reasonable and "doable," only the people who actually must make the changes can really decide if they can all be done. That is why in choosing an implementation plan it is always best to limit yourself to a few key actions and objectives for the short term.

Implementing a Plan of Corrective Action. How will the benchmarking team's recommendations be achieved? Do you have a plan for carrying through what has been proposed? These are more than idle questions because without a detailed plan of action the team's proposals are merely a kind of wish list. In order to make the changes happen, you need a set of goals specifically selected to correct the deficiencies that have been identified. The objective of a detailed, documented action plan is to accomplish those goals by integrating the benchmarking study's results into your organization. Such a plan should consist of the end goals and the tactical steps or process changes that are required to accomplish the goals, adjusting both the organization's short-term and long-term plans as needed. Although the benchmarking team, senior management, and the people who will implement the actions might reach agreement on a set of tactical (short-term) actions quite easily, the proper solution to close the gap may require a strategic (long-term) action. Because strategic actions require more significant commitment, change, and resources, they are usually more difficult for management to accept. This is why consensus is so vital. Unless there is a clear strategy (one that can be communicated, monitored, and measured) that management and the process owners have bought into, the value of what you have learned might well be lost. Some of the questions the plan must answer are the following: Is the direction clear? Do all the stakeholders (the benchmarking team, management, process groups) know who is going to do what? How will decisions be made? How will progress be measured and monitored?

Responsibility for Managing and Recalibrating

In approving the implementation plan, senior management is responsible for ensuring that the team has built into the plan the roles and responsibilities of all the persons who will have to contribute to its success. Of course, the annual performance measures and reward systems that support the new goals will also need to be revised. Most important, someone will have to be responsible for managing the implementation plan and assuring that it stays on course. But a plan is only as good as the efforts to check its progress, which is why there have to be regular reviews of the action plans. The plan's manager must establish a schedule for tracking events and milestone measures. If there are no specific means to measure the major milestones or a schedule for inspecting the plan's progress, for all practical purposes the outcome is being trusted to chance. In order to avoid this, some kind of project management tool should be used. Finally, any experience—even a failure—is a source of new knowledge and provides sagacity for taking new risks. To take advantage of this kind of learning, while you are doing the monitoring you will also want to plan for follow-up benchmark studies (that is, recalibration). Such follow-up studies will let you know if you are staying current with your partners. At the same time, inspections of your benchmarking progress will test your understanding of your process and your learning. Also important to impress upon the rest of the organization the significance of benchmarking in the pursuit of best practices are inspections, obtaining feedback during the process rather than waiting until the end. Managers have to learn, as Dave Kearns advised, "to become coaches by inspecting the steps used to accomplish the results" (Kearns and Nadler, 1992, p. 233).

The Final Report

A major milestone in any benchmarking project is the final report. The final report generally consists of a written document and an oral overview of it. Although either one may precede the other, it is more common for the written report to come first. Regardless, as has already been noted, neither a published report nor a formal presentation should come as a surprise to the stakeholders. Senior managers, process owners, and affected employees should all have had an opportunity to participate in the development of the contents. Experience shows that the most successful approach to organizing a final benchmarking report is to divide it into three sections: an executive summary, a description of the study process, and, of course, a thorough review of the findings.

Executive Summary. The purpose of an executive summary is to give the reader a quick overview of what the team learned and what they believe the organization should do to respond to the findings. By definition, a summary is succinct, an outline, not a lengthy exposition. A summary must also be clear to the reader; therefore, it should focus on the performance gap and your projection of its effects on the organization. The executive summary should highlight the key results of the study, the team's conclusions, and its consensus on recommendations, including action planning. By structuring the summary to highlight these points, you will force the reader to address the main points of the study at the very beginning. Many senior managers haven't the time (or the patience) to be briefed on extended processes—they want to know the bottom line at the very start. This is what the executive summary does. Still, the next two sections of the report (discussing the methodology and findings) must be sure to present the full logic behind the team's recommendations.

Study Process. The study process section describes the study's methodology. It presents the basic data along with some elaboration on the following key points: how the benchmarking subject was chosen, how the partners were selected, how the data were gathered, what information-gathering methods were used, and your analysis technique. This section should include an outline of the steps taken from beginning to end along with a calendar of events. In reviewing your research, be sure to identify all of your data sources along each step of the process. Be thorough. Include all publications, databases, individuals contacted both inside and outside the organization, uses of reverse engineering or process reconstruction, and so on. The process review should describe how the project team was selected and why. Be sure to identify all the people who were involved directly, including the indirect support personnel with their titles. In your discussion of the partner selection process be sure to cover all the analysis that was used in the final list determination; explain why some organizations were not selected or why other potential partners chose not to participate. Finally, review the study or data-gathering methods you used, such as telephone interviews, site visits, and so on.

Findings. This is the section of the report in which you present what you have learned and the plan you propose to implement to make use of that learning. Begin by highlighting the data you have gathered and presenting them in terms that are as clear and concise as possible, emphasizing the study's purpose statement and what you have learned. Tying the findings to your purpose statement will be a salient feature for your audience to focus on. If your audience has endorsed the purpose statement, you will win their attention by showing that the findings are an outcome of pursuing the study's purpose. The key is to show the gap between you and your partners and explain it against the backdrop of your current practices. Using graphics to clarify your points, your goal should be to convey what you have discovered. Next, expand on the recommendations you reviewed in the executive summary. You can do this by listing your recommendations and matching the tasks and resources needed to accomplish the necessary changes. In addition, review the implementation schedule and its key milestones, explain who will be responsible for the plan, and suggest how progress will be monitored. The intent of this section is to gain consensus for your plan.

The Live Presentation

Presenting your data in the best possible way to a live audience requires careful thought and planning. As already suggested, the makeup of the audience and their involvement in and knowledge about the study and the conclusions the team has reached will influence the presentation's structure. Also consider how much briefing you have provided the audience and whether the written report has already been produced and distributed. I cannot state too often that you want to delay a live presentation until you have been able to brief the audience on the study, your recommendations, and how they and their organizations will be affected. You and your management champion must always do what is necessary to avoid surprises during the presentation. When the members of your audience take their seats you want them to be positive about you and your benchmarking study. At the very least, you want them to be intrigued by what you are about to present.

Structuring the Presentation.

Keep in mind that your audience will include people with varying levels of knowledge about the study, familiarity with the effects of your recommendations, and interest. This diversity is certain to affect attention levels and, hence, data retention. In addition, attention levels are likely to fluctuate during your presentation. However, what your audience remembers is the best measure of your presentation's success, so be aware that some sections of your presentation will be remembered more than others. In addition, many factors—such as time, room arrangements, proclivity of your audience, the handouts—will also have an impact on the audience's reaction and memory.

The literature on presentations usually suggests breaking them down into three parts—the introduction, the body, and the wrap-up or conclusion (Morrisey and Sechrest, 1987, p. 40). However, for the purposes of a benchmarking study, the live presentation, like the written report, may be thought of as including an executive summary, a review of the study process, and an expanded report on your findings. Once again, because senior managers today have little time to waste (and have grown accustomed to being presented the bottom line first), a summary is important to help them grasp quickly the major issues of the study and the investments that will be required. Again, it is best if they have already been briefed well enough that they are inclined to your recommendations; nevertheless, the summary section of your presentation is another opportunity for you tell them why your benchmarking study was needed in the first place and why the organization should make investments in the recommendations.

Once you have organized your data into an effective structure—one that reflects your study, conveys your honest conclusions, meets your objectives, and satisfies the needs of your audience—the next questions are when and where to make the presentation.

Scheduling. When you schedule the presentation try to make it at a time that is convenient for the majority of your audience. For example, avoid conflicts with other events. Also, pick a time when your audience will be open to your message: although asking for incremental funds is never easy such requests fare better when they occur during the budget-setting process. Of course, you may have to make your presentation during a regularly scheduled staff meeting, which may place limits on the timing and process of your exposition. When this is the case, it is a good idea to contact the person responsible for organizing the staff meetings so that you can become more familiar with the layout of the meeting room and try to influence the agenda so that your presentation is given the best possible time. Find out also what the customs are regarding meeting process and expectations of speakers. This is the staff's playing field and you will have to grapple with the house rules, so it is best to know them in advance.

Handouts. Increasingly, organizations today are using handouts as a means to update meeting participants on subject matter, meeting process, and purposes and to clarify expectations. When handouts are supplied in advance, handouts during the presentation may not be necessary. Such preliminary material usually consists of the written report (or an abstract of it). It is supplemented by one-on-one meetings that prepare key participants for the study results and recommendations.

Even with this kind of preparation, many benchmarkers still find handouts during the presentation useful. Handouts are a common and effective aid in benchmarking presentations because they can provide explicit data such as technical information, evaluation procedures, and process flowcharts in a handy format. However, if prepared in a careless manner, they can appear improvident or even endanger a presentation's effectiveness.

Handouts have three basic uses during a presentation: to reinforce key points or data; to summarize actions that you want the audience to follow up on; and to add supporting data that don't fit well as visual aids.

Once you have decided which handouts would be most helpful, decide when you will distribute them. Obviously, you have three options. You can hand them out right before you begin the presentation, during the presentation, or after the presentation.

Before the Presentation. The difficulty with distributing handouts before your presentation begins is that your audience may start to satisfy their curiosity about the contents while you are speaking—and when people are reading, they are not listening. One way to deal with this problem is to have the handouts already on the seats when the audience enters the room. This will give them time to read before you begin speaking. You can also explain the substance of the handouts at the beginning of your presentation, thus satisfying the audience's curiosity about the contents at the outset.

During the Presentation. This is the most difficult of the three options. If you decide to distribute handouts during your presentation you will want to do it in a way that minimizes the interruption to your presentation's flow. Therefore, do it quickly and at a time when the handouts are relevant to the point you are making. Unless you are careful, the handouts will be a distraction from your presentation rather than an aid. An appropriate handout to give out during a presentation might be a detailed financial analysis that amplifies the trends you are reviewing. Also appropriate would be a description of a new work process that several pages of charts would help the audience to understand more fully.

After the Presentation. Probably the least disruptive option is to forgo distribution of handouts until after your presentation is completed. During the presentation you can tell your audience that handouts that explain the point you are making will be available after you are done. This will let them know that they don't have to try and copy down each slide you show. The drawback of this approach is that many people like to add notes to the handouts during a presentation. In addition, the lack of backup data may lead to unnecessary questions of clarification.

Audio and Visual Aids. With or without handouts, there are certain to be a few key messages in your presentation that you will want to emphasize or elaborate upon. A number of means can help you create such images. The medium you chose will depend on several factors, including the size of your audience, the length of the presentation, the amount of preparation time available, the facilities, and the cost. George Morrisey and Thomas Sechrest (1987, p. 72) report that overhead projectors and transparencies are used in about 60 percent of all business and technical presentations, another 20 percent are supported by 35-mm slides, and the remaining 20 percent use "flipcharts, handouts, props of one sort or another, computers, video recordings, or combinations of all of the above." Today, portable Powerpoint presentations projected onto screens from laptop computers are being added to the mix. Regardless of the medium you use, its effectiveness will be diminished if it is not adequately seen or heard or is hard to use. In addition to the size of the room and the audience, consider if any in the audience have hearing or sight impairments, if the room is subject to outside noises, if the seating arrangements present visual obstacles, and if the lighting is appropriate. Steve Mandel (1988, p. 25), a consultant who specializes in presentation skills, offers some guidelines for the use of visual aids.

Mandel suggests using visual aids to

- Focus the audience's attention
- Reinforce your verbal message
- Stimulate interest
- Illustrate factors that are hard to visualize

He cautions not to use visual aids to

- Impress your audience with detailed tables or graphs
- Avoid interaction with your audience
- Make more than one main point
- Present simple ideas that are easily made verbally

Getting Started. The best place to begin your presentation, as the old saying goes, is at the beginning. Jump right into your subject in order to impress a busy, time-constrained audience. To get started without delay, consider an opening like the following:

> Good morning. Expenses and productivity are important topics for our organization, especially as our company strives to constrain overhead spending. Today I want to show you why our training expenses are out of line with other organizations in our industry and what we can do about that situation in the next three to six months.

Follow this up right away with facts, wasting no time or words. Basically, present your key point in the first few minutes of your talk. People like to know what your purpose is, even if they've been briefed in advance. So tell them what you hope to accomplish, why you're making this presentation. Here's an example:

> The reason we're here this morning is to find out how we can reduce training expenses by 15 percent in the next six months while making better use of our facilities and staff. Why is this important? Because if we make better use of our staff and facilities we can provide the same levels of training support to our sales and service organizations with less effort and expense, thus making a positive impact on our return on assets. That means reducing the company's expenses and improving the profit sharing payout to all of us. So our purpose this morning is clear: how to improve training delivery more effectively with greater rewards for us all.

As has been noted earlier, during the body of your presentation you are likely to get questions or encounter resistance to your data or your conclusions, especially from those most threatened by the study or its results. When that happens, do not become emotional, and never take the opposition personally. Here are some of the tacks you can take in responding:

- Provide more information.
- Draw a comparison with something familiar to the audience.
- Present your argument gently; redirect your listener's reasoning, invite him or her to reexamine a personal motive or belief.
- Ask a question to clarify your listener's reasoning.
- Use humor, but not at the listener's expense.
- Cite an outside authority—your partners, for example—or your own experience.
- Admit you don't know the answer and offer to find out.

Persuading an Audience. Bill Repp, an independent consultant and the president of Organization Development Group, advocates the following methods to get an audience to buy into your ideas:

- *Appeal to them on a basic level.* Identify their needs and show how your idea or proposal will meet those needs. For example, explain how they can save money, how much money they can save, when they'll save it, and what they can do with it.
- *Present ideas in terms of current beliefs.* It's rare when we are convinced to do something or believe something that doesn't conform in some way to our present value system. Therefore, phrase what you say in such a way that it confirms what they already believe.
- *Use the "yes response" method.* Begin your presentation with a series of propositions that people can readily agree with and accept easily, things to which they'll automatically say yes. Keep making these kinds of statements, then show how they can continue to say yes to your idea. (Salespeople think in terms of overcoming objections and presenting the benefits of their products.) People signal agreement with either a word, a smile, or a nod of approval.
- *Use the "this or nothing" approach.* Show what it will be like if the company doesn't accept your proposal. If you're proposing the purchase of new equipment, show what will happen if the organization doesn't buy it. For example, sales will go down, employee turnover will increase, customers will continue to be disappointed, and so on.
- *Use solid facts and vivid illustrations.* People don't buy abstract ideas, such as "economy," "beauty," or "comfort." They buy a proposed savings of $500. So tell stories that will illustrate your ideas. Help people visualize your ideas. Describe them in concrete terms, what people can see, touch, feel, smell, or taste.

Summary. Here's a final review of my advice about presentations before live audiences:

- Be prepared.
- Rehearse, rehearse, rehearse.
- Be confident.

- Speak slowly, using plenty of pauses and short sentences.
- Watch your audience; keep eye contact and be aware of unrest.
- Stay on track.
- And once again be prepared, and rehearse, rehearse, rehearse.

Integrating the Study's Results into Operations

Organizations that have a successful track record with benchmarking studies know their power to motivate employees. These organizations have learned that employees will support productivity improvements and changes in their work processes when they have reliable data to compare their own operation with a better performer. The lesson in this for managers is that when the changes you implement are based on realistic assessments they invariably lead to significant performance improvements. This is true because focusing on the practice allows the organization to understand what kind of gap exists between it and the industry leader. Once the gap is clearly understood it is almost always obvious to the people familiar with the work what should be done to close it. But this will not happen on its own. The organization will certainly have to adjust its performance goals and perhaps its operational targets and strategies. To make sure that the direction is understood and accepted, employees need the support of new expectations and performance measures and perhaps additional resources and process-change assistance. They also need reminders and recognition for their progress. Greg Watson (1992, p. 83) calls this support the "three Es—enablement, empowerment, and encouragement."

More and more organizations are utilizing benchmarking as a corporatewide, comprehensive, controlled, and continuous part of the planning process. These organizations recognize that in the new economy, information is strategic, but it is also fast-moving and free-flowing. Not long ago a researcher at the Stanford

Research Institute (SRI) coined the term *gold collar*. He meant that in addition to traditional blue-collar and white-collar workers, a new kind of employee is emerging—the gold-collar worker—so called because he or she possesses strategic knowledge. When such people leave an organization, they take with them its strategic advantage. In an environment where products and production ideas are the outcomes of input by many people, it is difficult to maintain advantages. Therefore, it is becoming important to maintain contacts and exchanges with one's current and future competitors and to be open to new ways of doing things. Leading-edge organizations have learned that in our global and aggressively competitive marketplace they must continuously and determinedly work to weed out weaknesses and replace them with strengths. The not-invented-here syndrome has given way to benchmarking as a strategic tool for prioritizing investments and activities.

Traditionally, an organization's goals derive from its mission, objectives, and operating principles. The business planning process usually starts by communicating the mission, goals, objectives, and operating principles throughout the organization for understanding and commitment. These goals are documented in the formal business plan and from this plan, strategies and action plans develop. The business plan is reviewed and approved by senior management and supported by an operating budget. But today more organizations are building benchmarking into the planning process because the goals based on benchmarking findings, which reflect current realities of the marketplace, are usually enthusiastically accepted by middle management. In these organizations operating plan approvals include commitment to benchmarking studies and use of their findings. Plans and target performance are built into the performance appraisals and recognition and reward processes and senior management reviews inspect progress toward benchmark goals. Most significant, benchmarks are recalibrated as part of the annual business plan update. (I will discuss this further in the section on monitoring the action plan.)

When you are determining the best way to incorporate bench-marking into the planning process, keep in mind the three kinds of benchmarks. Here's a review of them:

- *Performance benchmarks*. Performance benchmarks are used to set and validate objectives for an organization's key performance metrics in the short term and the long term. To achieve this goal, planning documents should consistently report benchmark perfor-mance metrics that are reasonable projections of benchmark per-formance improvement rather than benchmarks based on current performance.
- *Process benchmarks*. Used to plan for business process improvement, process benchmarks should be documented as part of the relevant functional business plan. They should be an inte-gral part of improvement projects that support achievement of the organization's planned strategies.
- *Product benchmarks*. Product benchmarks are used to aid product planning and development. Product documentation should thoroughly and consistently incorporate product perfor-mance goals and design practices identified through benchmarking in product documentation.

Taking Action

The success of your action plan will be contingent upon your orga-nization's creativity for solving challenging problems. When a benchmarking study has disclosed a gap between you and a partner, the challenge you face is to develop new practices or process changes for those activities and tasks that are lagging. In addition to fixing the process problem, the changes you propose will have to assure that any new responsibilities, roles, and rewards are clearly stated. The starting point is the reexamination of the organization's current goals on the basis of the data from the benchmarking study. The purpose is to adjust the organization's short-term and long-term plans to accommodate the new goals. Of course, the annual performance measures and reward systems that support the new goals will also need to be revised. Finally, some kind of project management tool should be used and when appropriate one of the four methods of implementation decided upon, as discussed later in this chapter.

Benchmarking organizations know that when the changes they implement are based on realistic assessments, they will lead to significant performance improvements. By focusing on the practice the organization is able to understand the kind of gap that exists between it and the industry leader. And when the gap is clearly understood it is almost always evident to the people familiar with the work what has to be done to close the gap. But as I have said, this will not just happen. The organization has to adjust its performance goals, its operational targets, and its strategies. To assure the new direction is grasped and accepted, employees need to see the new expectations and performance measures as part of the organization's traditional management processes. Therefore, functional goals based on a benchmarking study should be established in the same manner the organization would ordinarily enact its operating objectives and performance measures.

Establishing Functional Goals

Most benchmarking organizations begin their replanning process by reexamining current goals against the benchmarking data. Then they adjust their long-range plan to accommodate the new annual goals that have been selected to reach the benchmark. Many organizations also find it necessary to revise their annual performance measures and reward systems so that they support the new goals, especially when it comes to process improvement. This is significant because when you concentrate only on results, that is what employees will do: they will focus on results rather than on improving the process that produces the results. This is why managers who are experienced in implementing benchmarking results go out of their way to provide recognition and rewards not only for results but also for the quality and integrity of the work process that produced the results (Schmidt and Finnigan, 1992).

To facilitate this replanning process many benchmarkers find that it helps to put the external findings into "operational terms," that is, to use the language of the function that will have to change, quantifying the benchmark in such a way that it can be easily adapted. It is also helpful to determine the more significant benchmark measures from the more trivial. As already noted, this can be done by ranking those that will make the greatest contribution toward closing the gap. But always remember that while the metric or measure shows how great the gap is, where it is, and how often it shows up, the practice itself has to be understood if it is to be changed. If you only have numbers and don't know what they mean or why they exist you won't be able to craft goals. Once the practice is both well understood and measured, management and the people who will have to implement the changes can get behind the new goals.

You will also find that some resistance to benchmark findings will be diffused when they are converted into planning statements. As an example, statements like "provide competitive levels of customer satisfaction by market segment," "reduce unit costs," and "increase inventory turns" are nonthreatening because they are not specific to any single organization, position, or person. For this reason, planning statements can be discussed openly and understood across organizational boundaries, making the integration of benchmarking results into the planning process easier.

Developing Action Plans

To achieve its objectives, an organization must have a plan of incremental actions that lead to the ultimate goal. Winning the game may be the goal but unless individual players can master their opponents, play by play, action by action, the goal will remain illusive. A plan of tactical action allows an organization to map out the tasks that individual employees and teams must accomplish if they are to establish the new work processes, performance stan-dards, and results.

In developing actions for specific work groups the focus is on two areas: the tasks that have to be completed (what has to be done, how will it be done, who will do it, and when it must be done) and the behavioral changes that may be necessary.

Task Planning. For many this is known as Management 101 because it refers to the planning steps of task accomplishment, which has been the subject of many books. For our purposes, there are five considerations in task planning:

- *Purpose of the task and expected results.* When the task has been accomplished what will have happened? The task should be described in complete detail so that there is no misunderstanding about what has to be done and how you will know when it has been done. Often the task description may require more detail than the findings from the study.
- *Sequence of events and schedule.* What are the steps that have to be taken in order to complete the task and when must they occur? These steps should be fully described, put in the proper, log-ical order—even broken down into subelements—and prioritized. Start and stop dates should be developed. Any interdependence on other task plans should also be identified. There are many tradi-tional means to track such plans (for example, Gantt and PERT charts) and also many software programs available.
- *Resources.* What resources are needed to complete the task? Resources include manpower, budget, equipment, staff support, input from other groups, and management time for review and guidance.
- *Responsibilities.* Who will do what has to be done? Who will provide support? How will accomplishments be measured? Each responsibility should be known and accepted by each of the partic-ipants. If a subsegment of a task is contingent upon the work of another person or work group, this should be spelled out and the

appropriate person held accountable. Also, each step in the plan must have a measure that can be used to determine if it was completed.

- *Monitoring of progress.* How will progress be measured, who will do the measurement, and when and how often? Each step has to have a specific measurement, and there must be a plan to inspect work in progress.

Behavioral Considerations. Perhaps the most common mistake managers make in assigning tasks, especially to subordinate managers, is failing to consider whether those responsible for the task are committed to making it happen. They may be able to do the task, but will they do it? Perhaps the best way to assess an individual's or a team's behavioral capabilities is to use *force field analysis*. Developed by Kurt Lewin to help groups facilitate change, force field analysis allows you to look at the relative priority of factors on each side of a balance sheet. Figure 5.1 presents an example.

The figure illustrates a force field that Warren Schmidt and I developed to identify the five helping factors in managing organizations and the five blocking factors. A manager launching a specific task or a full range of tasks can follow this method to assess the strengths of his group to accomplish the task and the weaknesses that will work against achieving it.

The Action Plan Process Capability

Will your plan succeed? Will it produce what you expect? In developing an action plan an organization's creativity for solving problems is extremely important. But it is also important that the plan produce the desired results. Defining the new practices and process changes will increase the chances for the plan to succeed, as will clear roles and responsibilities. There are also a set of key questions managers should ask before implementation to assure that a plan will work:

Figure 5.1. Management by Fact.

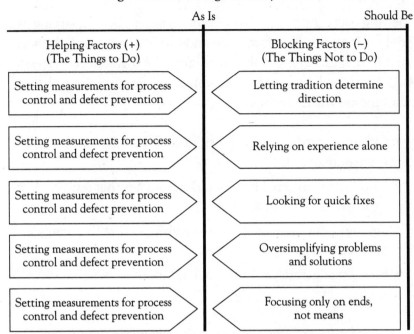

Source: Schmidt and Finnigan, 1993, p. 92. Copyright 1993 by Jossey-Bass Inc., Publishers. Used by permission.

- Do you have agreement from all the stakeholders that the new practice is the correct action to take? Are the benefits to the new practice known, and can their value be shown to the stakeholders?

- Will other work groups help with implementing the plan? Do they know and accept their roles?

- Have you selected the best site for the first implementation? Are there other sites that might be better?

- Is the timing right? Are there any major events or deliverables on the calendar that might interfere with the implementation?

- Can the implementation be pretested or simulated to guarantee a successful change strategy?

Gaining Acceptance

Getting everyone in the organization to accept benchmarking as a tool for improving performance and productivity has to be a key goal if integration is to take place. Some of the actions successful organizations have used to reinforce the importance of benchmarking are the following:

- Communicating a clear description of the practice and how it is measured.
- Conducting internal benchmarking studies that lend credibility to an external study's findings.
- Taking operational people on site visits so that they can see firsthand the practice in action.
- Engaging operational personnel in follow-up benchmark studies.

In order to encourage acceptance of benchmarking, you want the organization to strive for an optimal end point—a state when benchmarking is recognized and accepted as an integral tool of the organization. The best way to characterize this for your employees is to define exactly what you mean by both the desired state and the current state. In this way your people will understand the changes that are necessary. For example, you may want an organization in which benchmarking has been institutionalized. But your current organization has no benchmarking activity, much less an understanding of the benchmarking model. In this case, a plan of benchmarking education and promotion would be seen as appropriate. Or it may be that in the current organization there is no ownership for the organization's practices whereas in the desired state you want full ownership of practices as well as recognition of the practical steps that are necessary to implement them. Again, once you know what the future should be, the right actions are more apparent. (See Table 5.1.)

Table 5.1. The Desired State of Benchmarking
in an Organization.

Present State	Desired State
Need for benchmarking not recognized	Acknowledged need for industry best practices
No benchmarking activity; no understanding of the model	Benchmarking institutionalized
No understanding of industry best practices	Full understanding of benchmarking practices
Competitive performance gap unknown	Understanding of differences in current and benchmark practices
No ownership of practices	Ownership of practices

Implementing Plans and Monitoring Progress

To be certain your plan does what you want it to do in the time frame you wish, some method for monitoring the plan's implementation and progress toward the achievement of the new goals has to be built into all of the organization's vital business processes, including the planning and management review processes. For example, changes in tactical action plans will necessitate changes in the current operating plan, and certainly functional or strategic action plans will have to be adjusted. Amendments to the individual performance assessment plans of particular managers and employees are also likely to be necessary. This is why there will have to be regular reviews of the action plans. Finally, as part of your efforts to monitor the plan and its progress, you will need to plan for follow-up benchmark studies. The purpose of these studies is to be certain you are staying current with your partners because it is very likely your partners will continue their efforts for improvement. Such inspections of your benchmarking progress are also important to underscore the importance of benchmarking to your organization both in the setting of performance targets and in the pursuit of best practices.

Without a carefully crafted implementation plan that includes monitoring guidelines and scheduled progress reports, the changes you desire may prove to be elusive. Establishing goals and milestones, integrating the review of these plans into normal operations reviews, and conducting formal inspection of benchmarking activities are all essential to success. But without monitoring support, your task will be much harder. And there also has to be a plan to *recalibrate* the benchmark, that is, reevaluate and adjust your benchmark.

Implementation Alternatives

Traditionally, management has advocated two methods for implementing action plans.

Line Management. This method is best when the plans and responsibilities are well understood, efficiency is important, and the work practice is under the manager's control. The drawback to this method is that it takes time away from that the manager usually devotes to supervising the operation.

Project Management Team. This approach calls for the establishment of a program team that is separate from the operation's line management to oversee implementation. This works best with large complex projects where there are important interproject and interfunctional considerations and dependencies and where effectiveness is the issue. The team will need special expertise and time to complete the implementation.

Both of these traditional methods can be successful. However, benchmarkers have discovered two nontraditional methods that work well with implementation of benchmarking findings.

Process Leader. This person can be responsible for ownership of the process when there is no other empowered person high enough in management available. It works best for processes affecting customers, like order entry, billing, and collection. When a process leader becomes responsible for ownership of the process, he or she must have access to cross-functional resources.

Work Process Teams. Teams are best when they have the capability to refine and adapt the benchmark practices as part of their own work process. When it is essential to gain active participation and support early on in the implementation plan, a work process team is best.

Monitoring an Action Plan

Monitoring an action plan is essential to getting the results you want. Dave Kearns used to say that one should "expect what you inspect." As I have stated, because inspection of the action plan is such an important part of benchmarking, it is best accomplished by integrating benchmarking right into the organization's key business processes like planning, management process, technology delivery, and so on, to ensure that everyone knows what is expected. Writing in Arthur D. Little's publication *Prism*, Herman J. Vantrappen and Phillip D. Metz (1994, p. 33) support this approach: "Purposeful action comes about only when communications channels are open and the spectrum of performance indicators is compatible with the technology and innovation priorities that the company has chosen to pursue. Continuous interpretation, learning, and adjustment are necessary to make sure that the scores on the performance indicators stimulate innovation in a direction that reinforces the company's competitive position."

Clarity and simplicity in the early stages of a benchmarking effort are important. This is why the organization's senior managers should limit their benchmarking labors to a few critical strategies, products, or business practices and center the organization's attention on them at each plan and operations review. It is more important to make consistent reviews of progress in a few vital areas than to cover a much larger number less frequently. First, senior managers and their direct reports should agree upon the critical metrics and processes that will be subject to continuing benchmark review; these should become standard agenda items in every review. As part of the monitoring process, benchmark performance metrics should be required in the plan and operations reviews and in the product design reviews.

Strategic Resource Redirection

Once your action plans are clear, the next step is to implement them. This will certainly require resources. However, rather than gaining incremental investment, it is likely that management will have to redirect existing resources. These kinds of trade-offs are never easy to make. But management has to ask itself what the cost to the organization would be if the action plan is not implemented. Benchmarking is never without some cost. However, organizations often discover to their pleasure that the costs of carrying out a benchmarking study and implementing its recommendations are offset by savings incurred by decreased waste or scrap, increased productivity, or fewer costs associated with replacing lost customers.

Recalibrating

Finally, in order to be certain that the data you have on your practices are based on the latest methods and the measures it is necessary to routinely reevaluate and adjust your benchmarks. Xerox (Camp, 1989) uses the term *recalibration* to describe this process. Such a reassessment should be conducted before further benchmarking studies are performed. A recalibration effort should take place no more than eighteen months after the original study. It consists of two elements. First, follow up with your partners (at least the benchmark leader) to validate that the practice has basically not changed, that your gap projection is valid, and that the metrics you used are still cogent. Second, conduct an internal assessment of benchmarking, including surveys and interviews with the study participants, managers, and employees who have been implementing the action plan. The purpose of this internal assessment is to understand how effective the plan is, how the new practices are being received, and how people feel about benchmarking as a tool for improving productivity and work processes. Your internal assessment and the data you gather from your partners—and in particular the benchmarking leader—should provide you a good report card on the effectiveness of the original study.

Concluding Thoughts

The business world is undergoing fundamental change, and no organization or manager can stop the momentum. Providing the right response at the right time has become a competitive imperative for all organizations. It takes courage to think boldly in order to meet such challenges. Of course, businesspeople have always scouted their competitors, but now benchmarking is a recognized management specialty, based on aboveboard data-gathering techniques.

The final phase of the benchmarking model is to internalize your study's results and launch the action plans that will close any gaps between you and the benchmarking leaders. Identifying which of your goals will have to change, communicating this direction clearly, and monitoring your progress toward the new goals will ensure an effective close to your study.

Benchmarking is important to all managers because no longer can self-improvement opportunities be based on internal comparisons to set and measure goals. In the global marketplace, it is imperative that your organization measure up to world-class standards. Benchmarking is the tool for this and the pursuit of productivity.

Part Two

The Long-Term Payoffs
of Benchmarking

Chapter Six

Organizational Effectiveness

Achieving Breakthrough Change Through Simplified Processes

> If you wish to understand what Revolution is, call
> it Progress; and if you wish to understand what
> Progress is, call it Tomorrow. Tomorrow performs
> its work irresistibly, and it does it from today.
> —*Victor Hugo*, Les Miserables

In the waning years of this century productivity has become the password to prosperity and adding value has become the focus of productivity-minded organizations. In the new global economy, value is added when there is knowledge creation, waste elimination, and little unproductive work. In other words, first, are we doing the right things? And second, are we doing things right? Organizations that do this have three characteristics:

- They have an intense desire to understand the market environment in which they operate and what their customers truly value.
- They identify and document the key internal business processes required to deliver that value.
- They have a commitment to the continuous measurement and improvement of their business processes to assure that those values are always delivered.

In this new era, productivity improvement is the result of managing end-to-end business processes because productivity gains are structural in nature and not easily sustained. The task is difficult but not impossible. Business processes that both create value and achieve productivity improvements can only be maintained if they are assessed within a comprehensive context of four spheres of competitive intelligence.

- *Technology.* The organization must know its current technology skills and future needs and provide a continuing opportunity for learning.
- *Competition.* The organization must identify its competitors and establish benchmarks that can be regularly reviewed.
- *Customer service.* The organization must know customer requirements and establish excellence in customer service.
- *Corporate culture.* The organization must maintain a "breakthrough" mentality by empowering employees, building teams, and rewarding success.

Management must remember that breakthroughs don't need to be complex. Rather, they are usually well within sight of the people who do the work. Let me share with you how a seemingly complex problem was solved with remarkable simplicity. It is the story of a nuclear power plant. The plant had two critical—and identical—switches that had been placed side by side. Although they looked alike, the two switches regulated the plant's reactor control rods in critically different ways. In fact, pulling the wrong one would instantly lead to disaster. The operators knew that regardless of what might be happening around them, they had to be able to recognize the difference between the two switches at all times (something that the plant's designers should have fixed). The operators' solution to the problem helped avoid the almost unimaginable costs of such a mistake in a nuclear plant. Yet it was simple, functional, and inexpensive: the operators merely placed easy-to-identify markers on each. On the rod control switch, they attached a Heiniken beer tap handle label. On the partial rod control switch they hung a Michelob label (Hoffer, 1988).

This is a good example of what the goals of productivity and process simplification (reengineering) are all about: uncovering new ways of engineering products and services and the work processes that make these processes and services more compatible with how people actually work. Although the key to true productivity is to find methods that eliminate errors and minimize their effects, the real success stories are those organizations that can implement the very best methods without impeding their capacity to learn new ways of doing things.

Empowering people to do what they inherently know is the right thing—using their own innovation, judgment, intuition, and brain power—is the key enabler in the drive for productivity. Empowered employees are fundamentally changing organizations throughout the world. They are changing their processes by building their knowledge base and integrating it with others to improve their productivity. It is benchmarking that is the key to uncovering new ideas for these employees, and it is an environment of trust that encourages the simplifying of their work processes by measuring what was produced, not how much was produced.

Effectiveness Versus Efficiency

Benchmarking increasingly is being used to help organizations define change strategies in their quest to achieve organizational effectiveness. Organizations grappling with such change are digging into their own and others' work processes to learn more about the relationship between work group design and effectiveness. They are doing this to understand better how resources, technology, and performance measures can be used to improve their work groups' effectiveness. They want to discover ways to work smarter.

Why the emphasis on process and business simplification? Although productivity is the result of efficiencies within an organization, efficiencies are almost always the result of effective processes that have been improved through simplification. Once an organization has decided to pursue productivity improvements by process simplification it learns that it has to move from internally defined benchmarks to end user–defined benchmarks. The old expression "There is no such thing as a free lunch" reminds us that we have to pay a price for everything we do. For one thing, every organizational process costs something and, for another, determining how a process can be simplified is not a unilateral act. The beneficiary of the work process—the end user—is best qualified to determine if a process is valuable and worth paying for.

Making a process simpler—that is, more effective—means reducing its complexity. Processes tend to become more complex and less effective when the process owner adds steps to deal with external errors or adapts steps to correct errors in the process itself. Experience shows that by eliminating internal and external errors an organization can produce extensive gains in productivity that far exceed any gains that might be made by improving the efficiency of an error-ridden process. In other words, automating an assembly process that is chock full of errors will create a crisis for everyone involved. Thus, implementing just-in-time manufacturing techniques without first eliminating or reducing current quality problems will only mitigate current difficulties.

Eliminating external and internal faults is a two-part process that produces exponential gains:

- Error reduction eliminates some process steps, such as disposition of faulty material, and reduces the number of times that some process steps, such as rework, have to be repeated.
- Once fewer rework steps are performed, there is less chance for internal errors. This, in turn, reduces the number of lower-level rework steps. Fewer rework steps at the lower level lessens the chance of internal errors once again and therefore reduces the number of rework steps at a still lower level, and so on.

By reaching beyond mere efficiency and striving for true effectiveness, many organizations have realized major productivity gains. By benchmarking with these organizations any manager can gain insights into reducing errors that will lead to the elimination of work at multiple levels of a process and in turn produce highly leveraged productivity improvements. David Carr and Henry Johansson (1995) identify several typical core processes: product and process design (time to market); research and development (concept to commercialization); order fulfillment (order sign to delivery or installation); conversion (raw material to product); procurement (sourcing to receipt); logistics (factory to customer); materials management (factory to retailer); and supply chain (material source to customer).

Productivity and Business Improvements

To be a productivity leader an organization has to maintain a constant search for ways to simplify its work processes. To do so, the entire organization must be focused on eliminating confusing, redundant, and otherwise unnecessary steps from current work processes. It must be clear to everyone in the organization that work process improvement is everybody's responsibility and that no one is in a better position to improve a job than the people who do the work on a daily basis. Ronald Moen and Thomas Nolan (1987, p. 68) said it well: "Improving product or service quality is achieved through improvements in the processes that produce the product or service. Every activity and every job is part of a process—and can be improved. Improvements come through people learning."

Thus, the quest for productivity begins by empowering employees to focus on work process improvements by doing things differently or eliminating them entirely. When the value-added concepts of total quality, and the customer's desire for timeliness, accuracy, and relevance, are added to today's cost-centered, volume-measured standards, productivity is within the reach of any organization. General Electric (GE) recently discovered this at its Appliance Park facility in Louisville, Kentucky, where it is building a new washing machine in a process that is an unprecedented departure from its normal practices. Working with a one-team process, "marked by first names and an informal dress code," and an outsourcing program, its "process has been the most cost-effective and quality-focused effort in its washer-manufacturing history" (Ettorre, 1995, p. 33). GE's Louisville experience is part of its commitment to achieving processes and cycle times that are better and faster than those of any other company in the world. There are three keys for GE and other organizations in reaching world-class productivity:

- Recognition of the need for breakthrough improvements in business processes
- Employee empowerment throughout the organization
- Technological excellence

Organizations like GE have also established measures for all the outputs of their key business processes. To support a drive for productivity, these measures must reflect multiple views of productivity—those of customers, internal stakeholders, and investors. Measures also must allow for in-process inspection and correction and make it possible to know when world-class productivity has been achieved.

Flowcharts

Of course, you can't improve something if you don't know how it works. Therefore, organizations have to document their business processes, both to understand their impact on the customer's requirements and to highlight opportunities for improvements. The most efficient way to do this is with flowcharts (see Chapter Two). Each work group should scrupulously illustrate every phase and step of their processes with a well-constructed flowchart. In describing GE's process document experience, Tichy and Sherman (1993a, p. 251) reported: "Some process maps were so complex that they covered whole walls and resembled diagrams of the wiring in computer chips. The maps noted even such seemingly minor matters as the signatures required to approve purchases or shipments. Since a document tends to sit on a desk for a day before it's signed, cutting out a few unnecessary approvals can significantly speed up a process (when process mapping failed to help, it usually was because the attention to detail got out of hand)."

A flowchart provides a work group a forum in which to create a common awareness of what the group does and how it can apply problem-solving techniques and other productivity improvement efforts. Everything the group does is part of its process. If something is not adding value then it's undermining value and probably producing some kind of waste. Waste includes overproduction, wasted time, unnecessary transportation, extraneous processing, excessive motion, and errors or defects. But the failure to solicit, accept, or recognize the ideas of others may be the greatest waste of all.

Benchmarking and Productivity

Without benchmarking, organizations that aspire to top productivity will find that it alludes them. This is so because benchmarking helps determine the most important practices to improve and the best approaches to use in doing so. Organizations around the world—including your business competitors—are focusing on productivity improvements to achieve higher rates of return and superior customer satisfaction. Gaining an advantage over competitors is benchmarking's mission. Remember, to implement a productivity improvement strategy an organization has to rally its employees to focus on the effective use of work.

Organizational Change

Organizations are constantly changing in today's world of rapidly changing technologies, takeovers, "arrangements of convenience," emerging nationalism, and global competition. It is no secret that the frequency of the changes affecting our organizations and the level of energy required to react to them is intensifying. Peter Vaill

(1989, p. 115) describes it as trying to survive in a "permanent white-water society," where there are no quiet pools for recouping energy and perspective.

To survive, companies are constantly adjusting to the market-place, public policy, and society. When something goes wrong with a product or a competitor does the unexpected or a new environmental regulation is enacted, management acts to put the system back into balance. Changes are made in policy, strategy, or operating principles, but basically what management does is simply restore the organization to the state it was in before the problem occurred. However, anyone who has tried to make significant changes in an organization knows that doing so is a difficult task. In their book *Benchmarking for Best Practices*, Christopher Bogan and Michael English (1994, p. 180) developed a model to show the relationship of the four kinds of change organizations can pursue: continuous improvement, managed reform, organization restructuring, and BPR. Their model shows how these four approaches differ in the degree of change they represent. (See Figure 6.1.)

The model's vertical axis shows tactical or strategic change. Tactical changes are small improvements, such as process changes that reduce product rejections. Strategic changes are much larger, such as accelerating time to market by 50 percent. The model's horizontal axis depicts the longevity of the change, either immediate or extended. Immediate change is as fast as one to three months; extended change takes months or even years to occur (a BPR project may require two or three years to complete). When performance improvements are measured against these two dimensions, four possibilities emerge.

Immediate Tactical Change (Continuous Improvement)

Immediate tactical change involves daily, weekly, or monthly improvements. In Madison, Wisconsin, a team of workers and

Figure 6.1. Performance Improvement Methods.

		Velocity of Change	
		Immediate	Extended
	Tactical	Continuous Improvement	Managed Reform
	Strategic	Organizational Restructuring	Process Reform

Degree of Change

Source: Bogan and English, Benchmarking for Best Practices, 1994. Used by permission of the McGraw-Hill Companies.

managers looked for easily identifiable problems for which they could find workable solutions, fix the problem, and move on without studying the underlying causes or the overall system that might have contributed to it. For example, they set out to cut vehicle turnaround time from nine days to three days and save $7.15 for every dollar invested in improvements, which resulted in an annual net savings of $700,000 (Schmidt and Finnigan, 1992).

Immediate Strategic Change (Organizational Restructuring)

Immediate strategic change entails functional transfers, structural reorganizations, downsizing, and realignments. Organizations around the country have made short-term productivity gains and saved on expenses during the past ten years through restructuring and downsizing. At the same time, organizations are pursuing *extended* or *virtual* structures by outsourcing services that were traditionally provided by their own work forces. For example, Xerox recently contracted all of its information management (IM) services to EDS, including the transfer of its IM employees to EDS's payroll.

Extended Tactical Change (Managed Reform)

Extended tactical change consists of a multitude of reactive and proactive management actions to reduce or eliminate errors or negative trends and to ensure that operating processes meet management objectives. At Solectron Corporation, for example, customers submitted a weekly "report card" on four key factors, giving them an A (100), B (90), C (80), or D (70). At 7:30 each Thursday morning, the top management team—including the division managers—met to see if the scores were 95 or better. When the target was met week after week it was hard to see much chance for improvement. However, this changed dramatically when management lowered the weighting of the letter grades: A (100), B (80), C (0), D (–100). The target remained 95 or better and a manager receiving less than 95 had one week to report what was being done to correct it. After this new procedure was implemented, the average project rejection rate dropped by half.

Extended Strategic Change (Process Reform)

As the term implies, extended strategic change refers to an extensive set of activities for evaluating processes and procedures, organizational structures, and the application of technologies in order to reinvent the way an organization conducts its business. Xerox has embarked upon a strategy to achieve world-class breakthrough productivity by effective utilization of people, simplification of processes, and elimination of waste. Strategic and annual plans are developed against specific productivity goals, based on the two basic enablers of their productivity pursuit: business process improvement and people empowerment.

To compete in the new economy you must take risks, be bold, and have strong leadership. You must anticipate customers' needs, giving them not just what they want but what they will learn to want. Ken Blanchard (1994, p. S38) says: "Learning is inevitable in the future. Change is coming so fast now that people must constantly retool and rethink the things they're doing."

Building a Learning Organization

Learning and the acquisition of knowledge are at the heart of growth and development in today's global economy. Facilitating and accelerating the unleashing of your employees' know-how and creativity is the key challenge of the new economy and the knowledge revolution. Being able to assimilate and comprehend knowledge more easily is the great promise of the digital era. But first organizations must accept that knowledge drives growth. To succeed today, an organization must realize that people possess knowledge and have answers and that by providing timely context, releasing knowledge, sharing ideas, and building knowledge, an organization can drive innovation. And it is innovation—through new products and services, new processes, and new knowledge—that drives growth.

The challenge is in what an organization does differently: how it changes the way it works and what it works on as a result of what it learns. Learning to leverage employee knowledge and intellectual capital helps create new value, which in turn allows you to provide customers new and different services and solutions instead of just doing the same old things faster and cheaper. Organizations that want to grow into the new century will have to deepen their understanding of knowledge work. At the 1992 Presidential Economic Conference in Little Rock, Arkansas, Paul Allaire, Dave Kearns's successor as CEO of Xerox, said: "We need to undertake massive retraining of our current work force. This is something that only we in industry can do. It will only be accomplished by on-the-job training, by workers learning from each other and learning from their involvement with the work."

Most organizations tend to be concerned with labels, wanting a name for each of their experiences. In itself, this is fine—accountability is important! But we have to learn that some knowledge cannot be categorized, labeled, or named. It flows like a river through our unconscious, shaping who we are and what we become. This is the deeper realm of learning that experience brings to life. Edwards Deming, one of the founders of the quality and continuous improvement movement, gave a name to the ability to use and apply continually what we already know in a way that has never been done before. He called it *profound knowledge*.

Much has been written about learning organizations. The most notable work is Peter Senge's *The Fifth Discipline* (1990) and his definitions and analysis are widely quoted. But perhaps the simplest and easiest definition of the learning organization is the one offered by Nancy Dixon of George Washington University: "The intentional action of an organization to continuously transform itself through both adaptive and innovative learning" (Calvert, Mobley, and Marshall, 1994, p. 40). I like that, but we also have to remember that learning is driven by need and accessibility; that is, we learn what we need to learn when it's needed.

Bogan and English (1994, p. 18) identify five behaviors that characterize learning organizations:

1. They train employees quickly and effectively to foster new learning, shrink error rates, and accelerate program, product, and service rollouts.

2. They attract fast-learning employees who are responsive, receptive, and resilient.

3. They leverage past successes—and failures—to improve their processes and services continuously.

4. They adapt quickly and—because they listen closely to customers—innovate rapidly.

5. They concentrate on reducing cycle times and simplifying processes.

Recently, a series of human resource development focus groups discussed the criteria for learning organizations (Calvert, Mobley, and Marshall, 1994, p. 40): "Learning organizations employ a distinctive set of learning strategies and tactics. Their learning differs from that of other organizations; for example, in its effectiveness, productivity, adaptiveness, and link to achieving goals." They went on to say that the term *learning organization* describes "an organization that excels at advanced, systematic, collective learning." In contrast, *organizational learning* refers to methods of collective learning. This distinction in meaning suggests three useful, if debatable, conclusions:

1. All organizations learn. (In other words, all use organizational learning methods.)
2. All organizations learn at different levels of proficiency and at different paces.
3. To become a learning organization, an organization must find ways to make learning more intentional and systemic.

Learning from Mistakes

Helping workers learn from their mistakes is a key part of the new learning and the new management style. By learning more about their work processes, employees and managers are increasingly able to learn from their mistakes. Most breakthroughs in work activity result from insight gained through personal experience. Many organizations are discovering that if they can institutionalize this phenomenon they can anticipate significant improvements in work processes and technology development. For example, both Martin Marietta and Xerox have all their engineers meet at the completion of a project to capture lessons learned and share this information with other teams. In an era where intellectual property is the most important and where white-collar and blue-collar workers are fast being replaced by gold-collar workers (those who have strategic knowledge), it is important for organizations to facilitate the transmission of knowledge to as many workers as possible in the shortest time possible.

Learning from Others

New benchmarkers are always astonished and humbled by the willingness of others, especially those involved in the quality movement, to share. The reason they share is that they are proud of what they do. Of course, there is also some initial resistance because most of us have a lot of psychological baggage to discard before we can successfully learn from others. Perhaps the greatest fear is of being seen to be "copying." This is because from grade school on, we are discouraged from working together and rewarded for achieving individually. But benchmarking is much more than copying because it requires deep self-assessment and the ability to translate practices that work in another context into an appropriate process for one's own organization.

Although benchmarking is an effective learning tool, some organizations resist it for fear of losing a competitive advantage by sharing information. Although no organizations should share proprietary information with competitors, in the knowledge economy the realm of proprietary advantage is quite small. The few islands of competitive advantage are surrounded by oceans of opportunity in business and management processes. Competitive advantage is in speed and quality of execution and deployment, not proprietary information.

One learning method is site visits. On any given day, hundreds of groups of managers are walking through someone else's plant or office, asking questions as they occur and expressing delight and appreciation at what they see. Interesting? Yes! Entertaining? Almost always. Productive? Only if you are lucky. This industrial tourism is a far cry from the deep analytical work that really needs to be done to adapt and adopt the best practices to your situation.

Training and Traditional Learning Methods

The primary learning assets of any organizations are its traditional methodology for learning, whether this involves in-house resources or purchased services. These kind of investments are often considered to be overhead rather than investment opportunities. Any organization that aspires to be a learning environment must accept the value of providing its people knowledge. For example, executives at Motorola estimate that the company reaps a return of $33 for each dollar it spends on education. They also contend that at least 5 percent of each employee's time should be spent on training or education (Waterman, Waterman, and Collard, 1995, p. 91).

Stephen Gill (1995, p. 30) has identified four keys to unlock the power of learning:

1. Link training events and outcomes clearly and explicitly to business needs and strategic goals.

2. Maintain a strong customer focus in the design, development, and implementation of all training activities.

3. Manage training with a systems view of performance in the organization.

4. Measure the training process for the purpose of continuous improvement.

Behaviors Vital to the Learning Organization

A manager who wants to adopt the personal practices that will lead to a learning organization must first focus on those few vital behaviors that will best help to achieve this goal. At the same time he or she will have to be aware of the behaviors that will block progress. A manager can do five things to create a learning organization:

1. *Treat training and learning as a required investment in human assets.* Learning does not occur without costs. A smart organization will certainly invest in developing or acquiring training programs and give every team the time to attend this training. But much more is required! To be successful a manager must see the members of his or her team as assets whose value to the organization can be replenished over and over again. This includes including time for learning in the work day.

2. *Encourage people to learn from mistakes.* In an environment that encourages prudent risk taking, some failures can be used as valuable learning experiences. When they are reviewed in the right perspective, failures are a rich ground for learning that can lead to

significant breakthroughs in process improvement and technological development. Failures should be studied and analyzed, not punished, to enhance the probability of future success.

3.   *Identify, catalog, and publish organizational learning resources.* Managers are "servant leaders" who want to enable their teams to be more productive. To do so they have to provide a compilation of information regarding the technical, management, and quality learning opportunities available to their organizations. Because it is certain the team will require educational support beyond that available inside the organization, managers have to help the team diagnose the special needs of their work processes and facilitate the acquisition of this learning. They may simply provide access to information about customers, work processes, or variances in production or they may offer technical skills and knowledge that can only be acquired by cross-training or through an outside learning program.

4.   *Make everyone aware of core competencies.* One of the hallmarks of total quality is the consistency with which processes and tools are applied within the organization. With consistency, everyone from the boardroom to the shop floor, from engineering to marketing speaks the same language. To achieve this kind of consistency, all of an organization's people must be trained according to a set of core modules (such as a quality improvement process, problem solving, and statistical tools) that support the practice of quality improvement in their job. When an employee's work environment requires specialized technical skills not needed by the majority, relevant skill training should be provided for those employees alone.

5.   *Use process improvement as a learning tool.* How an organization deals with its problems tells much about that organization's values. Understanding one's work process not only builds the knowledge to improve the process but also provides the confidence for action that comes from knowing what to do. This also recognizes that powerful learning takes place within the work group on the job.

One obstacle to transforming an organization into a learning organization is that such transformation means broad and sweeping change. It takes a long time. Employees can become disenchanted and stop doing the right things simply because they do not have the patience to see it through. But you have to believe it's worth the struggle. Once we understand what we need to know, we can help define it. When we can define it, we can model it. Then we can do it and communicate it. Finally, we can take ownership of the idea of knowledge-driven work and learning.

Concluding Thoughts

There is today an increasing emphasis on leveraging employee knowledge and intellectual capital to create new value. This is why it's important to do new and different things, especially through services, instead of just doing the same things faster and cheaper. Benchmarking will continue to influence and shape the future of organizations even more as we move toward the next century. It will provide organizations with the information they need for extending their understanding of knowledge-based work and deepening commitment to performance improvement.

When an organization truly understands its core competencies and uses business process reengineering and learning to improve its productivity, it can pursue customer service with the confidence that it can compete with anyone. John Byrne (1995, p. 132) provides some sage advice about the quest for productivity: "Modern managers are wise to learn from other companies willing to share their ideas, but they can't forget that all the tours in the world aren't going to give them the competitive edge they need to survive and thrive. It still comes down to the obvious: produce a product people want at a competitive price and you will succeed. Simple as that idea may be, however, the path to true enlightenment is never easy."

Chapter Seven

Strategies for the Future

Key Competencies for the New Economy

> Skate to where the puck is going, not where
> it's been.
>
> —*Wayne Gretzky,*
> Wayne Gretzky: An Autobiography

I began this book by pointing out that in the developing global economy, an ability to compete is no longer sufficient. Rather, business organizations need to stretch beyond themselves to define new products and markets that haven't even been conceived of yet. But how can companies create their own successful futures? First, they must learn from their environment—the best and brightest competitors, markets, products, and processes in their industry. Then they must broaden the definition of their environment to include other industries. In the new global economy the process of constantly scanning the environment for best practices is imperative and the responsibility of every manager who wants his organization to grow and thrive.

Along the way to what many were already calling the second American century, someone changed the rules. The competitive advantage the United States enjoyed after World War II lessened while production capacity blossomed worldwide. The primary cause of this proliferation has been the rapid spread of new technology, which respects no national boundaries. Since basic materials have become available throughout the world, geopolitics is also undergoing some change, and the old geopolitical rules about resource heartlands no longer seem relevant. In addition, advances in communications and transportation technology have made it easy for multinational companies to serve large, homogeneous international markets from their home countries. Decentralized worldwide production and sales and reduced costs are facilitating industrializing nations to enter world markets at an incredible pace (Vernon, 1987).

In his book *Global Paradox,* John Naisbitt (1994, p. 16) says that as the world integrates economically, "The component parts are becoming more numerous and smaller and more important." In other words, as the global economy gets larger, the component parts get smaller. He likens it to the paradox in physics: "Bigger and bigger machines are being built to study tinier and tinier things" (p. 21). In organizations around the world, business units are becoming smaller in order to globalize the economy more effectively. According to Naisbitt, the mantra of the 1980s—"think globally, act locally"—has been turned on its head.

Also, knowing the effects of all these changes is difficult because so many causes are at work and so many effects are still not clear—it is like trying to identify the source of an echo from across a valley. Even after you have studied the hills and mountains around you and listened carefully to locate the source, all you are likely to ascertain is that the echo was launched from one of them; precisely which one is never clear. In *America and the New Economy,* Tony Carnevale probably did a better job than anyone in helping us understand why the world's economy is being fundamentally restructured. He gave the following causes (Carnevale, 1991):

- The increasing wealth of nations and workers
- The globalization of economic activity
- The diversification of consumer tastes
- The increasing value of time in a hurried world
- The commercialization of homemaking and personal care labor

- The increasing participation of consumers in production and service delivery
- Advances in technology

What Can We Expect of the New Economy?

It is too early to know what the long-term effects and outcomes of the new economy will be. We are, after all, still at the beginning of this economic and technological revolution. However, we are already experiencing some effects. For one thing, the turmoil over the apparently declining stature of American industry is more myth than fact. It may come as a surprise to some readers that the United States still leads the world in productivity. Averaged over the economy as a whole, for each unit of input the United States produces more than any other nation.

In February 1994 the U.S. government reported that worker productivity increased at a solid 4.2 percent rate in late 1993. To date in the 1990s, according to the *Los Angeles Times* (Peterson, 1994), productivity has been growing at about double the rate of the past two decades, fueled largely by manufacturing. By contrast, Japan has registered practically no advances in productivity since 1992, while Germany's labor costs have rocketed to almost twice the U.S. rate. The *Los Angeles Times* also reported a statement from Steven S. Roach, a senior economist at the Morgan Stanley Group Inc., an investment banking firm in New York: "Our competitive position is probably better than it has been at any point since the early 1960s."

Yet if these are supposed to be the good times, millions of American workers don't think so. In contrast to past recoveries, U.S. companies have been enhancing their ability to compete in the world by slashing payrolls, restricting hiring, and implementing laborsaving technology. In January 1994 alone, U.S. employers announced nearly 109,000 job cuts, the highest monthly total in at least five years. In 1993 U.S. employers announced 615,000 layoffs.

But the net effect has been to make the United States more competitive because America's economic rivals are just beginning this unpleasant exercise. "Germany is perhaps 10 percent of the way into this restructuring, while we're perhaps 75 percent to 80 percent of the way there," says Ross De Vol, an economist for the WEFA Group. "Japan is just starting to cope with it" (Peterson, 1994, p. A18).

There are some who believe that these economic gains have been made at a terrible social cost—rising unemployment and widespread anxiety about job security. Clearly, with such large-scale changes, people would be crazy if they weren't anxious. Robert Samuelson (1995), commenting in *Newsweek*, suggests that a heightened anxiety is not all bad. In fact, up to a point uncertainty compels organizations and workers to remain competitive. Samuelson says: "A society that accepts the inevitability of some insecurity may suffer less of it than one that avidly pursues absolute security. Gradual and modest change may avoid delayed and wrenching change. This is important because, at some point, the economy will cease to be boring. Something bad will happen: higher inflation, a recession, industrial turmoil. The impulse to ease the hurt, though natural, may be wrong. The lesson of our economics course is that a market society must often tolerate change, even unpleasant change, because the alternative is worse."

Despite the evidence of U.S. economic efficiency, two areas should still be closely watched. First, in product quality, service to customers, and speed of product development, American companies are no longer perceived as the leaders, even by American consumers, although there is evidence that the pendulum has swung in America's favor in some industries, including automobiles, copiers, and telecommunications. Second, in the recent past technological innovations have been incorporated into practice more quickly abroad while the pace of invention in the United States has slowed. Yet, again, recent evidence is positive. Although much has been written about the surge in U.S. patents awarded to Japanese

companies, less noticed is the fact that many U.S. companies—
from DuPont and Texaco to Philip Morris and Xerox—have
strongly stepped up their patent activity. Excluding special cases
like design patents, American patent winners have risen from a low
of 51.9 percent in 1988 to 53.0 percent in 1991 and 53.5 percent
in 1992 (Coy, 1993, p. 57).

The unpredictability of global economic events requires new
mechanisms for stability. Leadership and management practices and
investment in education and training are the factors that have
begun to determine the competitiveness of firms and countries.
Edward Baker (1990, p. 17) of Ford Motor Company said, "In order
to thrive, not just survive, in an explosive competitive environment, America's enterprises are faced with the simultaneous requirements of preventing change to maintain business as usual while
making the alterations needed to stay in business for the long term."
It is increasingly clear that the management challenge for the new
economic age is to involve all organization members in transforming and improving the systems and processes in which they work.

The process of economic progress is rarely smooth. As
Carnevale (1991) notes, the road toward the new economy nar-
rows as economic, social, technical, and political bottlenecks con-
verge. In previous economic transitions we have encountered
similar barriers and there is much to be learned from them—they
provide the context for our current economic dilemmas. How we
respond to these bottlenecks reflects our values as a nation and the
scope of our common sense in achieving an appropriate balance
between competing claims of public and private institutions,
employers and employees, and present and future generations.

Key Concepts of the New Economy

Many managers today look back longingly at the good old days
when managing meant "making the numbers." Today management
knows that a business cannot live by financial measurements

alone. In the new world of improved productivity, organizations are focusing on process improvement and employing wide-ranging performance indicators, both financial and other. As a result, managers have to learn how to manage complex systems and processes that involve many departments and functions.

In a *Harvard Business Review* article, Gary Hamel and C. K. Prahalad (1991) noted that the competitive battles of the 1980s were fought on the basis of incremental cost and advantages in existing, well-defined markets. They predicted that in the 1990s, the action would center on the battle to build and dominate fundamentally new markets. What Hamel and Prahalad described was a battle to create the future rather than to protect the past. Indeed, managers today are faced with a competitive paradigm based on an unknown future, rather than their past experiences.

We all must learn to do things in a new way. What new notions about the marketplace do managers have to consider? I believe that managers need to focus on six key concepts of the new economy:

1. Encouraging innovation and breakthroughs by establishing flexible strategies based on clear vision and direction

2. Identifying and capitalizing on core competencies

3. Developing and communicating organizational values and policies and creating an environment that facilitates organizational learning

4. Being open to partnerships

5. Recognizing that technology and services are merging and that markets that once were well defined now overlap

6. Realizing that organizations can no longer operate without understanding customer requirements

These concepts are discussed at depth in the remainder of this chapter.

Encouraging Innovation and Breakthroughs

It has become increasingly clear that new strategies must be flexible, based on an organizational vision that fully comprehends what the organization is and what it wants to accomplish. The old cliché about deciding if your organization is "in the buggy whip business or the transportation business" comes to mind. Plans must not be constrained by time, technology, or an unbending paradigm. But it is equally important to realize that in today's economy, a term like transportation may be too vague. Today's organizations must know who and what they are in specific, concrete terms so that they can capitalize on opportunities quickly and without major disruption. Xerox, for example, has redefined itself from a copier company to the "document company." By defining *document* in the broadest possible sense, the company can keep a firm grip on the office equipment market while positioning itself to promote technologies that enhance work effectiveness in whatever form *document* may take (Chakravarty, 1994).

Within a year of becoming CEO of Weyerhaeuser Corporation in 1991, John Creighton set out to revitalize his organization (Yang, 1995). He began by unloading units that were not core to Weyerhaeuser's mission, and more significant, by leading his managers through eighteen months of reengineering in which each mill and tree farm had to redesign the way it worked. His goal was to add $700 million to operating earnings by 1995. Measured in 1989 dollars (to eliminate the impact of price fluctuations in the cyclical industry), Weyerhaeuser met Creighton's goal a year early. Although $100 million came out of corporate overhead, most of it came from cost cuts and increased output at its plants. Many organizations, like Weyerhaeuser, are using reengineering to achieve performance breakthroughs. For example, Weyerhaeuser's box plant in Tennessee was losing money. After evaluating their work processes and tools, employees suggested buying used machines to speed production; within two years productivity per worker doubled (Yang, 1995).

Identifying and Capitalizing on Core Competencies

The skills, knowledge, and special abilities an organization possesses that set it apart from other organizations are its *core competencies*. Successful organizations in the new economy are learning to downsize to these core competencies while outsourcing nonessential roles. Many are restructuring according to core competencies rather than by products or markets. The challenge facing companies in the 1990s is to create value, both in their products and their organization. To meet this challenge, management must simultaneously improve a wide variety of initiatives such as quality, cost, cycle time, productivity, and profitability. At the same time they must devise new markets, new businesses, and a broad strategic direction. The only way to do this is to enhance the organization's capacity to leverage its resources. The most effective means to accomplish this is to build a strategy based on core competencies and core products.

Core competencies must not be confused with core technologies. Technology can be stand-alone (for example, the design of a very large laser printer). But competency transcends design capabilities (for example, consistently high printer reliability and low unit manufacturing cost). The process of converting good designs into high yields requires that multiple levels (for example, product assembly to product design) and multiple functions (for example, hardware and software engineers and manufacturing engineers) work very closely and effectively together (Prahalad, 1993). Nor should core competencies be confused with the core capabilities of an organization's groups, that is, its key processes. For example, just-in-time may be a special manufacturing capability or engineering may have some especially skilled ASIC designers. These are core capabilities. Although an organization's capability is crucial for its survival, unlike a core competency, it does not confer any unique advantage over other organizations. Identifying a core competency should be done carefully, by deliberate analysis and strategic planning. Too often organizations rush to judgment. Collis and Montgomery (1995, p. 124) note, "Managers often treat core competence as an exercise in intuition and skip the thorough research and detailed analysis needed to get the right answer."

To leverage core competency an organization must have competent people. Most core competencies are the result of cross-functional activities, requiring inputs from across organizational boundaries. This is because it is usually not possible to amass all the elements of a competency into a single organizational function and because competency cannot be managed in isolation from other people and skills. A core competency necessitates employee experts—groups of people with diverse viewpoints, training, ages, roles, and so on, engaged in real work, with real goals, using real tools over a significant period of time, in which they solve problems, learn and invent, and build things.

Developing Organizational Values and an Environment That Encourages Learning

Planning begins with a clear picture of where the organization is headed and how it will make the journey. By translating this vision of the future and the mission orders that will guide the transition process, an organization is able to establish clear goals and objectives and measurements to assure it will get where it is going in the most efficient way possible. Performance planning is not easy. It is tedious and trying. In addition, too many organizations write it off as the "soft stuff." But as someone once said, the soft stuff is often the hard stuff. In this case, it is essential.

An organization's vision provides a clear picture of a desired state that the organization wants to create. A vision statement presents the future in vivid color, depicting both its achievability and challenge. An organization's vision is senior management's optimism, emotion, and excitement for what could be. As Peter Block (1993, p. 115) notes about a great vision: "It comes from the heart and is unreasonable; we alone can make this statement. It is radical and compelling. It dramatizes our wishes."

When rapid turnaround and high quality are simultaneous customer demands, replicating successes and avoiding error are essential for survival. For these reasons, employees must be able to learn from their mistakes and their accomplishments. One of the major paradigms of the transition from the industrial era to the knowledge-based era is that intellectual capital must come before buildings and equipment. For one thing, intellectual capital has an increasingly shorter lead time and lifetime. In addition, in the new economy the information flow among people is more critical than the materials flow. Return on investment will increasingly have to be determined not on financial assets but on a return on expertise—the capabilities of an organization's individuals and groups.

Thus, around the world executives are gobbling up business books, hiring consultants, and paying attention to the expanding number of American success stories written by companies using innovative policies to motivate their employees. One such company is Allstate's Business Insurance Group in South Barrington, Illinois. To improve a paltry 2.9 percent return on equity, President Jack D. Callahan eliminated layers of management and installed incentive pay plans and self-managed teams in 1991 and 1992. The changes helped but not enough to meet Callahan's profit goals. So he took a page out of the book of another success story and followed the lead of Springfield Remanufacturing's CEO, Jack Stack, who was successful in engaging his employees in restructuring processes through an "open book" policy. Stack trained his employees to understand the company's financials and then shared them routinely with the work force, offering incentives for creative thinking in meeting goals. Callahan went on to do the same. He trained Allstate's thirty-five hundred employees to understand the importance of financial measures such as return on equity and provided them information on a regular basis. Callahan said, "It got employees involved and committed, and it gave them some ownership." The Allstate unit's ROE hit 16.5 percent in 1994 (Byrne, 1995, p. 128).

Organizations today must have reliable intelligence, not only about the marketplace but also about the organization and its competition. Naisbitt (1994, p. 99) says, "Winners and losers in the twenty-first century will be defined not so much by technological wizardry" as by the simple ability "to disseminate information where and when it is needed." Bob Buckman, founder and CEO of Buckman Labs, may have said it best: "As we move toward the chaos of the future, the progress of Buckman Labs relative to other companies will be determined by the growth in the value of knowledge that exists within the company. The acceleration of knowledge transfer is how we will grow this collection of individuals we call Buckman Labs into what it can be. Our strategic advantage lies in the leverage of knowledge" (Peters, 1994, p. 167). James Donlon, Chrysler's controller, said, "What you have to do is keep calibrating yourself to the world standard because it keeps changing. We're looking to keep our barometers sharp" (Ozanian, 1993, p. 53).

At the same time, successful organizations will invest in employee learning. This means a change in attitude on the part of America's corporations. As Thurow (1992) points out, what investment American firms have traditionally made in training is mostly concentrated on professional and management training, but this will have to change. More and more training dollars need to be spent on developing technical resources and the collaborative skills necessary to share such resources.

Being Open to Partnerships

Successful organizations are establishing alliances to help them fulfill their missions. Throughout the world, friends and foes are putting aside their differences and forming alliances and arrangements that would have been unthinkable just a few years ago. It helps to remember that many competitors outside of these arrangements are finding the going tough. Naisbitt (1994, p. 50) puts it very well in *Global Paradox:* "Competition and cooperation have become the yin and yang of the global marketplace. Cooperating is taking the form of a vast array of economic strategic alliances. Products can be produced anywhere, using resources from anywhere, by a company located anywhere, to a quality found anywhere, to be sold anywhere. This is being done through webs of strategic alliances. One of the reasons for the growth of strategic alliances is that companies are avoiding getting bigger."

Recognizing That Technology and Services Are Merging and Markets Are Overlapping

The only true predictor of market opportunity is the customer. *Technology push* has taken a back seat to *technology pull* and increasingly technology itself is secondary to solutions, which are what the customer wants. For example, home banking customers were initially technologists with home computers. But home banking has grown because of the number of banking customers who own PCs who don't have the time to go to the bank or write checks by hand. These customers are not technologists but ordinary PC users.

Realizing That Organizations Can No Longer Operate Without Understanding Customer Requirements

The customer must be involved in the design of products and services. At the same time, the time to get a product to market is dwindling and the life of products in the marketplace is shrinking. There is no longer any tolerance for error. Organizations must learn to deliver exactly what the customer requires. This can only be accomplished through some form of face-to-face dialogue between customer and supplier. Boeing is an example of an organization that has learned to listen to its customers. For example, in designing the new 777 airliner, Boeing engineers heeded American Airlines CEO Robert Crandall's complaint that a mechanic was needed merely to change the passengers' reading lights on an airliner. The new Boeing 777 will be the only jet in service on which a flight attendant can replace a reading light (Schmit, 1994).

To assess how effectively an organization's vision provides total value for its customers, Robert S. Kaplan and David P. Norton (1992) conceived a system called a "balanced worksheet." Their approach combines both financial and operational measures into an integrated system of performance indicators and is comprised of four elements:

1. *The financial perspective:* "If we succeed how will we look to our shareholders?" This perspective has three dimensions: profitability, growth, and shareholder value.

2. *The customer perspective:* "To achieve our vision, how must we look to our customers?" This perspective has four dimensions: time, quality, performance, and cost of ownership.

3. *The internal operating perspective:* "To delight our customers, what management processes must we excel at?" This perspective includes three dimensions: cycle time, quality, and productivity.

4. *The innovation and learning perspective:* "To achieve our vision, how must the organization continuously learn, improve, and create value?" This perspective focuses on innovation, continuous learning, and intellectual assets. It recognizes that many organizations today are building learning organizations for competitive advantage.

Concluding Thoughts

Organizations throughout the industrialized world are coming to see their enterprises as cross-functional webs of empowered work groups and using broad networks to manage their processes. Managers are discovering that their business processes are in need of reengineering if they wish to match fast-changing business demands. Increasingly these enterprises are searching for work flow designs that effectively connect their employees to sources of knowledge that provide value-added benefits to their customers. These managers are learning that reengineered processes offer potential for significant gains in productivity and that their redesign is increasingly based on the best work practices of other organizations.

Whatever the strategy chosen, the objective is still the same: organizational performance improvement. David Collis and Cynthia Montgomery (1995, p. 128) discussed this in a *Harvard Business Review* article: "Whether a company is building a strategy based on core competencies, is developing a learning organization, or is in the middle of a transformation process, those concepts can all be interpreted as a mandate to build a unique set of resources and capabilities. However, this must be done with a sharp eye on the dynamic industry context and competitive situation, rigorously applying market tests to those resources. Strategy that blends two powerful sets of insights about capabilities and competition represents an enduring logic that transcends management fads."

References

American Society for Training and Development. *National Report on Human Resources*. Arlington, Va.: American Society for Training and Development, July-Aug. 1992, pp. 1–3.

Baker, E. M. "Achieving Competitive Viability in the New Economic Age." *Readings on Managing Organizational Quality*. San Diego: Naval Personnel Research and Development Center, 1990, pp. 17–24.

Bean, T., and Gros, J. "R&D Benchmarking at AT&T." *Research-Technology Management*, July-Aug. 1992, pp. 32–37.

Blanchard, K. "The Future of Workplace Learning and Performance." *Training Journal*, May 1994, p. S38.

Block, P. *The Empowered Manager: Positive Political Skills at Work.* (expanded ed.) San Francisco: Jossey-Bass, 1993.

Bogan, C., and English, M. *Benchmarking for Best Practices: Winning Through Innovative Adaptation.* New York: McGraw-Hill, 1994.

Bowles, J., and Hammond, J. *Beyond Quality.* New York: Putnam, 1991.

Brooks, H., and Guile, B. *Technology and Global Industry: Companies and Nations in the World Economy.* Washington, D.C.: National Academy Press, 1987.

Byrne, J. A. "Management Meccas." *Business Week*, Sept. 18, 1995, pp. 122–132.

Caldwell, B. "Putting Technology to the Test." *Information Week*, Mar. 20, 1995, pp. 80–92.

California Manufacturers Association. "NUMMI Celebrates Decades of Work in State." *Sacramento Report*, May 20, 1994, p. 1.

Calvert, G., Mobley, S., and Marshall, L. "Grasping the Learning Organization." *Training Journal*, June 1994, pp. 38–43.

Camp, R. C. *Benchmarking: The Search for Industry Best Practices.* Milwaukee, Wis.: American Society for Quality Control, 1989.

Camp, R. C. *Business Process Benchmarking.* Milwaukee, Wis.: American Society for Quality Control, 1995.

Carnevale, A. P. *America and the New Economy: How New Competitive Standards Are Radically Changing American Workplaces.* San Francisco: Jossey-Bass, 1991.

219

Carr, D. K., and Johansson, H. J. *Best Practices in Reengineering*. New York: McGraw-Hill, 1995.

Chakravarty, S. N. "Back in Focus." *Fortune*, June 6, 1994, pp. 72–76.

Collis, D. J., and Montgomery, C. A. "Competing on Resources: Strategy in the 1990s." *Harvard Business Review*, July-Aug. 1995, pp. 118–128.

Colmen, K. S. "Benchmarking the Delivery of Technical Support." *Research-Technology Management*, Sept.-Oct. 1993, pp. 32–37.

Conference Board. *Benchmarking the Information Technology Function*. Report No. 1052. New York: Conference Board, 1993, pp. 1–22.

Coy, P. "The Global Patent Race Picks Up Speed." *Business Week*, Aug. 9, 1993, pp. 57–58.

Crosby, P. *Quality Is Free: The Art of Making Quality Certain*. New York: McGraw-Hill, 1979.

Crosby, P. *Completeness: Quality for the 21st Century*. New York: Viking Penguin, 1992.

Davidow, W. H., and Malone, M. S. *The Virtual Corporation*. New York: HarperCollins, 1992.

Day, C. R. "Lawyers Eye Benchmarkers." *Industry Week*, Nov. 15, 1993, p. 52.

Denton, D. K. "Lessons on Competitiveness: Motorola's Approach." *Production and Inventory Management Journal*, Third Quarter 1991, p. 23.

Dertouzos, M., Lester, R., and Solow, R. *Made in America: Regaining the Productive Edge*. Cambridge, Mass.: MIT Press, 1989.

Dobyns, L., and Crawford-Mason, C. *Quality or Else*. Boston: Houghton Mifflin, 1991.

Donnithorne, L. *The West Point Way of Leadership*. New York: Doubleday, 1994.

Dumaine, B. "The Trouble with Teams." *Fortune*, Sept. 5, 1994, pp. 76–82.

Ettorre, B. "GE Brings a New Washer to Life." *Management Review*, Sept. 1995, pp. 33–38.

Fitz-enz, J. *Benchmarking Staff Performance: How Staff Departments Can Enhance Their Value to the Customer*. San Francisco: Jossey-Bass, 1993.

Flanigan, J. "Numbers Can't Contain an Idea-Driven Economy." *Los Angeles Times*, May 28, 1995, p. D3.

Geber, B. "Benchmarking: Measuring Yourself Against the Best." *Training*, Nov. 4, 1990, pp. 36–44.

Gill, S. J. "Shifting Gears for High Performance." *Training and Development*, May 1995, pp. 25–31.

Gretzky, W., and Reilly, R. *Wayne Gretzky: An Autobiography*. New York: HarperCollins, 1990.

Groves, M. "A Road to Renewal." *Los Angeles Times*, Aug. 6, 1995, pp. D1, D6.

Hamel, G., and Prahalad, C. K. "Corporate Imagination and Expeditionary Marketing." *Harvard Business Review*, July-Aug. 1991, pp. 81–92.

Hoffer, W. "Errors on the Job Can Be Reduced." *Nation's Business*, Apr. 1988, pp. 33–35.

Hugo, V. *Les Miserables*. New York: Signet Classics, 1987.

Iacocca, L., and Novak, W. *Iococca: An Autobiography*. New York: Bantam Books, 1984.

Kaplan, R. S., and Norton, D. P. "The Balanced Scorecard: Measures That Drive Performance." *Harvard Business Review*, Jan.-Feb. 1992, pp. 71–79.

Karch, K. "Getting Organizational Buy-In for Benchmarking: Environmental Management at Weyerhaeuser." *National Productivity Review*, Winter 1992–1993, pp. 13–22.

Kearns, D., and Nadler, D. *Prophets in the Dark: How Xerox Reinvented Itself and Beat Back the Japanese*. New York: HarperCollins, 1992.

Kinni, T. "Best Practices Revealed." *Industry Week*, Dec. 5, 1994, pp. 30–32.

Kouzes, J. M., and Posner, B. Z. *The Leadership Challenge: How to Get Extraordinary Things Done in Organizations*. San Francisco: Jossey-Bass, 1987.

Kraul, C., and Iritani, E. "Asia, Mexico Learn to Work Together." *Los Angeles Times*, May 29, 1995.

Lee, M. "Firms Find a Better Way to Scout Out Competition." *Christian Science Monitor*, July 27, 1993, p. 9.

Lowe, S. "Learn from the Best: And Then Apply That Knowledge: The Pieces of Quality." *Democrat and Chronicle/Times Union*, Oct. 3, 1994, pp. 12–13.

Mandel, S. *Technical Presentation Skills*. Menlo Park, Calif.: Crisp Publications, 1988.

Manganelli, R. L., and Klein, M. M. *The Reengineering Handbook*. New York: AMACOM, 1994.

Marquardt, M., and Reynolds, A. *Global Learning Organization*. Burr Ridge, Ill.: Irwin, 1994.

Mather, C. V. *Winning High School Football*. Upper Saddle River, N.J.: Prentice Hall, 1955.

McConagle, J. "Benchmarking and Competitive Intelligence." *Journal for Quality and Participation*, Sept. 1992, pp. 30–35.

McNair, C. J., and Leibfreid, K.H.J. *Benchmarking: A Tool for Continuous Improvement*. Essex Junction, Vt.: OMNEO, 1992.

Miller, M. *Plain Speaking*. New York: Putnam, 1973.

Moen, R. D., and Nolan, T. W. "Process Improvement." *Quality Progress*, Sept. 1987, pp. 62–68.

Morrisey, G. L., and Sechrest, T. L. *Effective Business and Technical Presentations*. Reading, Mass.: Addison-Wesley, 1987.

Naisbitt, J. *Global Paradox*. New York: Morrow, 1994.

O'Brien, M. *Vince: A Personal Biography of Vince Lombardi*. New York: Morrow, 1987.

Ozanian, M. "Performance Measurement: Chrysler." *Financial World*, Sept. 28, 1993, p. 53.

Peters, T. *The Tom Peters Seminar*. New York: Vintage Books, 1994.

Peterson, J. "Economists Play 'Happy Days' as Many Sing Blues." *Los Angeles Times*, Feb. 21, 1994, p. A1.

Platt, S. (ed.). *Respectfully Quoted: A Dictionary of Quotations Requested from the Congressional Research Service*. Washington, D.C.: Library of Congress, 1989.

Prahalad, C. K. "The Role of Core Competencies in the Corporation." *Research-Technology Management*, Nov.-Dec. 1993, pp. 40–47.

Reich, R. B. *The Work of Nations*. New York: Random House, 1992.

Repp, W. "Effective Verbal Communications and Presentations." xSeminar workbook of Organization Development Group.

Richman, T., and Koontz, C. "How Benchmarking Can Improve Business Reengineering." *Planning Review*, Nov.-Dec. 1993, pp. 26–27.

Rummler, G. A., and Brache, A. P. *Improving Performance: How to Manage the White Space on the Organization Chart*. San Francisco: Jossey-Bass, 1990.

Samuelson, R. J. "Our Great Economics Lesson." *Newsweek*, May 22, 1995, p. 67.

Scheffler, S., and Powers, V. J. "Legal and Ethical Issues in Benchmarking." *Continuous Journey*, Dec.-Jan. 1992–1993, pp. 27–30.

Schmidt, W. H., and Finnigan, J. P. *The Race Without a Finish Line: America's Quest for Total Quality*. San Francisco: Jossey-Bass, 1992.

Schmidt, W. H., and Finnigan, J. P. *TQManager: A Practical Guide for Managing in a Total Quality Organization*. San Francisco: Jossey-Bass, 1993.

Schmit, J. "Jet Is New, and So Was the Process." *USA Today*, Apr. 11, 1994, pp. B1, B3.

Schulze, H. "HRD at the Ritz-Carlton." Paper presented at the American Society for Training and Development National Conference, Atlanta, May 11, 1993.

Schwarzkopf, H. N. *General H. Norman Schwarzkopf: The Autobiography: It Doesn't Take a Hero*. New York: Bantam Books, 1992.

Senge, P. M. *The Fifth Discipline*. New York: Doubleday, 1990.

Shah, D. "Interview with Dennis Dammerman, Chief Financial Officer, General Electric Company." *Human Resource Management*, Fall 1991, pp. 411–417.

Spendolini, M. J. *The Benchmarking Book*. New York: AMACOM, 1992.

Spendolini, M. J., and Thompson, N. H. "Benchmarking Etiquette." *Tapping the Network Journal*, Fall 1992, pp. 11–13.

Taylor, A. III. "GM's $11,000,000,000 Turnaround." *Fortune*, Oct. 17, 1994, pp. 54–70.

Thurow, L. *Head to Head*. New York: Morrow, 1992.

Tichy, N., and Sherman, S. *Control Your Destiny or Someone Else Will*. New York: HarperBusiness, 1993a.

Tichy, N., and Sherman, S. "Walking the Talk at GE." *Training and Development Journal*, June 1993b, pp. 26–35.

Toland, J. *In Mortal Combat: Korea, 1950–1953*. New York: Morrow, 1991.

Tucker, G., Zivan, S., and Camp, R. "How to Measure Yourself Against the Best." *Harvard Business Review*, Jan.-Feb. 1987, pp. 8–10.

Tully, S. "Why to Go for Stretch Targets." *Fortune*, Nov. 14, 1994, pp. 145–158.

Tzu, S. *The Art of War* (S. B. Griffin, trans.). New York: Oxford University Press, 1963.

Vaill, P. B. *Managing as a Performing Art: New Ideas in a World of Chaotic Change*. San Francisco: Jossey-Bass, 1989.

Vantrappen, H. J., and Metz, P. D. "Measuring the Performance of the Innovation Process." *Prism*, Fourth Quarter 1994, pp. 21–33.

Vernon, R. "Coping with Technological Change: U.S. Problems and Prospects." In *Technology and Global Industry: Companies and Nations in the World Economy*. Washington, D.C.: National Acadamy Press, 1987.

Waterman, R. H., Waterman, J. A., and Collard, B. A. "Toward a Career Resilient Workforce." *Harvard Business Review*, July-Aug. 1995, pp. 87–95.

Watson, G. *The Benchmarking Workbook*. Cambridge, Mass.: Productivity Press, 1992.

Watson, G. "Using Teams to Conduct Benchmarking." *Continuous Journey*, Dec.-Jan. 1992–1993, pp. 12–15.

Will, G. F. *Men at Work*. New York: Macmillan, 1990.

Yang, D. J. "The New Growth at Weyerhaeuser." *Business Week*, June 19, 1995, pp. 63–64.

Index